CONCEALED
FROM
CHRISTIANS
FOR THE GLORY OF GOD

THE 1611 KJV
THE KING JAMES BIBLE AUTHORIZED VERSION

G. JOHN RŌV

Copyright © 2019 G. John Rōv

All rights reserved. No part of this book may be reproduced, stored, or transmitted by any means—whether auditory, graphic, mechanical, or electronic—without written permission of the author, except in the case of brief excerpts used in critical articles and reviews. Unauthorized reproduction of any part of this work is illegal and is punishable by law.

ISBN: 978-1-4834-9434-0 (sc)
ISBN: 978-1-4834-9436-4 (hc)
ISBN: 978-1-4834-9435-7 (e)

Library of Congress Control Number: 2018913970

Because of the dynamic nature of the Internet, any web addresses or links contained in this book may have changed since publication and may no longer be valid. The views expressed in this work are solely those of the author and do not necessarily reflect the views of the publisher, and the publisher hereby disclaims any responsibility for them.

Scripture taken from the King James Version of the Bible.

Lulu Publishing Services rev. date: 02/14/2019

About The Author

It is most unfortunate that in the Christian demise of our day the church has patented spirituality and leadership and therefore "the truth," with formal education and most abhorrently to God, religious and professional titles. As a result, the stilted church is decaying from its emptiness within, lacking a spirit of razor sharp revelation and illumination and true transformation from the deep working of the cross and the Spirit by experience.

Ask yourself, when was the last time you met a Christian and walked away sensing the presence of another worldliness? A sense of absolute authority guarding and pointing you to the ancient and narrow paths which lead to the life? A sense that you have encountered meeting Jesus Christ Himself? A resulted awakening in you of fear and trembling from your own lack of the kingdom of God?

It is not the Lord's way for a man to need to put forth his credentials and qualifications (2 Cor. 11:17). It is enough to meet me in my words and ask the Lord and know. But if any man need proof of Christ speaking in me, I dare not put forth the spirit of the age and will only put forth the following, that I possess the genuine experiences in Christ which have wrought the truth in me:

Touching my history... I have been with Jesus.

> *Now when they saw the boldness of Peter and John, and perceived that they were unlearned and ignorant men, they marvelled; and they took knowledge of them, that they had been with Jesus (Acts 4:13)*

Contents

Preface ix

1	Concealed..	1
2	If Any Man Will...	4
3	Satan, The Self And The KJV...	7
4	Jesus, The Word Of God 1...	11
5	Jesus, The Word Of God 2...	15
6	Jesus, The Word Of God 3...	19
7	Jesus And The Nature Of The Bible 1	23
8	Jesus And The Nature Of The Bible 2	26
9	Jesus And The Nature Of The Bible 3	28
10	Jesus And The Nature Of The Bible 4	31
11	Jesus And The Nature Of The Bible 5	35
12	Jesus And The Nature Of The Bible 6	40
13	Jesus And The Nature Of The Bible 7	46
14	Man, The Cross, And The KJV...	52
15	A Body Hast Thou Prepared Me 1	57
16	A Body Hast Thou Prepared Me 2	62
17	A Body Hast Thou Prepared Me 3	67
18	A Body Hast Thou Prepared Me 4	71
19	A Body Hast Thou Prepared Me 5	77
20	A Body Hast Thou Prepared Me 6	83
21	Equality Or Truth?..	90
22	Born Upside Down...	94
23	Books..	98
24	Chapters	107
25	Verses..	117

26	Words	125
27	Letters	135
28	Numbers	141
29	The Year 1611	147
30	Prophecy	154
31	Trial	162
32	The Standard Lowered	167
33	Counterfeits	172
34	Preference Or Conviction?	178
35	Babel	181
36	First The Natural Then The Spiritual	186
37	Foreign Language Bibles	192
38	Bios	197
39	It Is Finished 1	200
40	It Is Finished 2	210
41	It Is Finished 3	220
42	It Is Finished 4	230

Postface 239

Preface

We cannot speak the history of the 1611 King James Bible without bringing up the name of William Tyndale. This man was a saint and a prophet of the living God.

A saint because his life work was this confession: "I defie the Pope and all his lawes. If God spare my lyfe ere many yeares, I wyl cause a boye that dryveth the plough, shall knowe more of the scripture than he doust."

A prophet because his martyrdom called in the King James Bible with his final words: "Lord! Open the King of England's eyes."

God honored Tyndale's life work and last will and testimony. Less than a hundred years after his death, through James, King of England, by the Holy Spirit's supernatural issuing of the King James Bible, his prayer was answered, exceeding abundantly above all he could ask or think. Today, the King James Bible, which contains very high percentages of Tyndale's word for word English translation of the Old and New Testament, has reached more boys that drive the plow than any Bible version in human history.

This book, "Concealed From Christians For The Glory Of God," is written in the spirit of William Tyndale, to illuminate the most foolish and nobody of believers to understand God's way of the scriptures (bibliology) more than the evangelical popes that fill the pulpits today, who deny the finished work of the Holy Spirit in the King James Bible.

There is no other book on this matter written like this book that I am aware of for the following reasons: First, this book strictly uses the King James Bible's own self-disclosure and nothing else. The KJV speaks for itself as the word of God; Secondly, this book is not written to explain to the carnal mind of the flesh, but for the eyes and ears of the heart of those who are looking for Jesus the Lord and Savior, to touch Him. It is written to make you a perfect man of God by reaching your conscience and healing your understanding of the Bible that God finished, rather than make you a scholarly intellectual; Third, this book is a spiritual book for spiritual men. As such, while verse context is important, context will not paralyze us from touching the prophetic spirit of passages. The Spirit wrote the prophetic Bible above all, and our Lord gave prophetic spiritual answers (Mal. 4:5; Matt. 11:14). This is the propositional way of the Lord regarding all things revelation, including His finished Bible, and this is what this book is after, and what all other books on the subject are missing, *"He that hath ears to hear, let him hear (Matt. 11:15)."*

Very few people begin a book and finish it. The reader who does so with this book and keeps what he hears will be rewarded. Because of the momentous building nature from chapter to chapter, if you will stay the course, you will not only have wisdom regarding the scriptures, but you will know God deeper in the ways He desires to be known, in spirit and in truth.

In chapter one we will take on the fact that God does indeed conceal from us even devastatingly important matters. Regarding these consequential matters, it is our privilege and not our right to be brought into the light of the truth.

In chapter two, we will confront our own willingness to believe something should God present it to us, notably, correcting our understanding of the King James Bible. We are not really listening to God (or God speaking to us through someone) if we are not truly willing to be changed by Him (or them).

In chapter three, we will see that the scriptures bear witness from the beginning of Genesis, that Bibles which do not issue out of the mouth of God are merely the wood, hay and stubble of man at best and the poison of Satan at worst.

Chapters four through six will lay ground work regarding the deep and mysterious oneness of Jesus, the Word of God, and the Bible, the word of God. In the two-foldness of God, what is true of one must be true of the other.

Chapters seven through thirteen will lay further ground work, this time regarding the nature of the seed and growth and maturity of Jesus, the Word of God, and the Bible, the word of God. We will see their identical nature according to the Father's laws of creation in time and manifestation from eternity.

In chapter fourteen, we will see that because of the oneness of Jesus, the Word of God, and the Bible, the word of God, not only is their nature identical but their ministry is also identical. Both needed to be physically present and pass through the suffering of the cross together and enter into resurrection life and power. Yes, the King James Bible was at Calvary.

Chapters fifteen through twenty will examine Jesus, the Word of God, who was made flesh, and the finished Bible, the word of God, which therefore was also made according to the human body.

In chapter twenty-one, we will see that if we are looking for an equal understanding regarding the true Bible, to be reached in the church by all, we will miss the truth. God is not a God of equality but the God of truth. Are you seeking the truth regarding the Bible?

In chapter twenty-two, we will see that we come from being upside down from birth in all our thinking. The idea that God has not finished a specific Bible but leaves it up to men is an upside-down thought and a shame to the church.

Chapters twenty-three through twenty-eight are pivotal. While the entire book narrows in on the King James Bible vs. other translations, a quantum leap takes place here. If nowhere else in this book, it is here that we must let Jesus catch us. He is the fisher of men and it is our loss if we are not caught by Him regarding His true Bible. Beginning with the wide scope of the books of the Bible, and narrowing in to the chapters, to the verses, to the words, to the letters, to the numbers, God forces us to deal with the miracles and wonders and signs of the King James Bible and answer the question, "at what detail point has God taken His controlling hand off of the process of the Bible from start to finish?"

In chapter twenty-nine, we will see that all modern Bibles confess the 1611 King James Bible as the true Bible according to what is shown on the cover of this book. This is prophecy, and the nature of prophecy is frightening because it is hard to see and scarcely believed.

In chapter thirty, we will see that the wholesale blindness of the church in our day to the authority of the King James Bible is also prophecy according to last days, and that we need to be saved from this prophecy of God. The English-speaking portion of the church was appointed by God as the pastor of the world and will be held accountable for casting God's finished Bible out of the church.

In chapter thirty-one, we will see that every prophecy once awoken to, is a trial. It is we who are on trial and not the King James Bible.

In chapter thirty-two, we will see the result in our day of removing one single word from the Bible. When the other Bibles were demanded, and God's finished Bible was officially rejected, the word *"sodomite"* came down, lowering the standard of the exact word out of the mouth of God, and the LGBTQ flood was able to come in. The church is responsible for this current condition and not the world.

In chapter thirty-three, we will see that counterfeit Bibles will always be patterned after the true word of God but lack the authority and power and authenticity as they do not source from Him. As a result, the church is in its weakest hour of existence and decline. The untold damage of counterfeit

Bibles will only be truly known on the other side and cannot be measured by our insensitivity to the matter or our false sense of security now.

In chapter thirty-four, we will see that our accolade of the KJV as a worthy translation, or even our preference of the KJV over other translations, is an insult to God and that only conviction that it is the very word of God will count as faith.

In chapter thirty-five, we see the obvious device of Satan to turn his upset at the tower of Babel back on top of the church and divide the church with far more than 100 English Bible versions, so that no one can agree on what is being said and blunt the testimony of the Bible to the world.

In chapter thirty-six, we see that the way for all men to pass into perceiving the spiritual identity of the King James Bible as the only true word of God which has proceeded from His mouth, is to first reject it out of the natural man before the Spirit's revealing reaches the spirit man. This is even as it is first for us to be deceived by Satan in our natural self before embracing Jesus as the only way and truth and life by the Spirit's revealing to our spirit.

In chapter thirty-seven, we deal with foreign language Bibles and lay out that while God's word is powerful in any language, they remain translations for good or for bad, and for better or for worse. They are necessary to bring in the gentiles, but they are not the inspired and inerrant final Bible of God. This reflects the strata of God's choosing, election and favor toward one man (the English speaker) over another (the foreign language speaker), in privilege and proximity to Himself. The flip side is the responsibility and culpability of the privilege and proximity to Himself in this matter.

Chapters thirty-eight through forty-five conclude the book with a brisk starter tour from Genesis to Revelation showing each of the Bible's sixty-six books corresponding in order to each of the sixty-six chapters of the book of Isaiah consecutively, according to the exact wording of the King James Bible finished word of God.

It is helpful to know that by the usage of the term "1611 King James Bible" I am referring to all versions of the King James Bible Authorized Version in a wider sense, since all versions of the King James Bible are the issue of the 1611 edition as they are the same in word and translation content, differing only in spelling modernization and type set from Gothic font to Roman text. Contrariwise, I am excluding and not referring to the New King James Bible.

I truly believe that any honest reader who neutrally and faithfully commits to reading this book from start to finish will become a whole-hearted believer that the King James Bible is the exclusive, perfect, authoritative, finished Bible from God… unless the reader is willfully or secretly to himself committed to unbelief. Welcome to the divine truth of the finished Bible that has been concealed from you for all this time for the glory of God, the 1611 King James Bible Authorized Version.

- G. John Rōv

CHAPTER 1

CONCEALED

IT IS THE GLORY OF GOD TO CONCEAL A THING: BUT THE HONOUR OF KINGS IS TO SEARCH OUT A MATTER

PROVERBS 25:2

God is awesome and greatly to be feared. It is a fact that this awesome God keeps secrets. In fact, He keeps them from us! And for this we ought to fear. Some of His secrets are of more consequence than others. When the Son of God entered the world as the son of man come in the flesh, this was an awesome secret. Actually, this secret was both concealed on many levels and in plain sight on many levels at the same time. For those who did not discover this secret the consequences were dire, even for some unto participating in His death. This thing was concealed for the glory of God (John 17:1).

Let's look at the God who keeps secrets:

The secret things belong unto the Lord our God: but those things which are revealed belong unto us and to our children for ever, that we may do all the words of this law (Deut. 29:29)

Here we see that God has secrets He keeps and secrets He reveals, and the secrets He reveals are in His word, *"law (vs. 29)."* However, even though we can say that God revealed the secret things of Christ in the word, *"law (vs. 29),"* to Israel, we have to also say that it was yet concealed to them still. After all, they thought that God revealed Christ to them but did not recognize Him when the time was at hand. You may be the same way as a Christian, on the one hand you say God has revealed to you that He wrote the Bible. Yet on the other hand, you really can't point to a Bible that you believe was written by God. Likewise, you do not recognize God's Bible at hand.

But thou, O Daniel, shut up the words, and seal the book, even to the time of the end: many shall run to and fro, and knowledge shall be increased (Dan. 12:4)

Here we see that God is passing secrets to one man in order for them to be kept for thousands of years to come. Through millennia the secrets would be trans-missioned to be revealed only to a last day generation. Not all of God's secrets are for revealing to all generations. We must pay attention to the generation we are in and uphold the Father's requirements for that generation. We certainly live in a generation that has the Bible completed which carries unique implications for us, not all generations could say this. That is what this book is about, "the Bible which bears God's seal."

He (Jesus) answered and said unto them, Because it is given unto you to know the mysteries of the kingdom of heaven, but to them it is not given (Matt. 13:11)

Here we see that God's secrets are based on His mysterious nature. This is so because the kingdom is the expression of the king. To reveal to some and to conceal from others is also mysterious. Of course, when Jesus said this He was speaking the words of the Bible. This means that the Bible is also very mysterious, and we must be carefully seeking God regarding it.

And when the seven thunders had uttered their voices, I was about to write: and I heard a voice from heaven saying unto me, Seal up those things which the seven thunders uttered, and write them not (Rev. 10:4)

Here we see an intensification of the topic of secrets concealed and secrets revealed. God is revealing to us that He is revealing to John alone precious secrets. There is also a similar experience in 2 Cor. 12:2-4 where God reveals to us that He is revealing precious secrets to Paul alone. Normally, it is not polite to tell a secret to someone in front of another person. By this treatment we know that God is very serious about concealing and revealing.

The secrets that God keeps are matters of divine revelation and require a prophet to reveal them. To understand the issue of God's authoritative Bible we do not need historians, manuscript experts, textual critics, or linguistic scholars but we do need the voice of a prophet. The word of God is this prophetic voice, and God will use it alone to reveal glorious secrets to you or to conceal costly secrets from you.

CHAPTER 2

IF ANY MAN WILL

IF ANY MAN WILL DO HIS WILL,
HE SHALL KNOW OF THE DOCTRINE,
WHETHER IT BE OF GOD,
OR WHETHER I SPEAK OF MYSELF

JESUS (JOHN 7:17)

This is the test then: Your will.

Are you willing to believe that the King James Bible is the finished word of God? This is a very simple question and a very pure question which bypasses your intellect and goes straight to your conscience. A good and honest heart will be able to immediately say that if God has finished the Bible in the King James Version, I am willing to believe on it so. You do not need to take anything into consideration to answer if you are "willing" to believe this.

It is very easy to see people struggle at this point when faced with the question, "Are you willing?" I want to reiterate what I stated above that there is no intellectual response for this question. We all know in our heart of hearts if we are truly "willing" to believe something or we are just giving the right answer of a Pharisee, a Sadducee, a Scribe, a Publican. Chiefly speaking, information is for the intellect, but divine revelation is for willing hearts searching for the truth: *"And ye shall seek me, and find me, when ye shall search for me with all your heart (Jer. 29:13)."* All truth is this way.

The more sacred a revelation of God the more it will cost to receive, if any man will. And without controversy, the sanctity of the Bible is held to the highest degree by God, *"thou hast magnified thy word above all thy name (Ps. 138:2)."* This sacred revelation of the King James Bible will cost you in the following: confessing your error; your reputation among Christians at large; your position in the academic world; your rank and pay as a teacher in a church or seminary; your ministry ambitions. Broken relationships are bound to occur. In many ways, your walk will be starting over.

But we should not be surprised that after being a Christian for so long there is still a pursuit ahead of us regarding the discovery of many divine revelations, such as the truth of the Bible. In the spirit of the simplicity of Christ we are asking very conscientiously fair and childlike faith questions:

- *Has God finished a Bible?*

- *If yes, where is it? We Should be able to point to it definitively.*

- *If no, at what point in history did God take His authoritative hand off of the Bible to leave man alone in the process?*

God Himself is fully capable of answering His children in all of the above. He does not need historians, manuscript experts, textual critics, or linguistic scholars, who strain to conjecture and carry no divine inspiration. These are not those He means when He says He has given the church teachers; for the perfecting of the saints (Eph. 3:11). His teachers teach all truth by His word in the spirit of apostles, prophets, evangelists and pastors. They have no need to go outside His word for answers to the above questions. They strongly know that His word is authoritative, and His word is sufficient, and His word is final for all matters of faith and practice, in this case, the doctrine of the scriptures.

When it comes to confrontations that require "if any man will," we must always pause ourselves no matter how much we think we know. We must not be so sure of our posture until we are absolutely ready to stand before Jesus Christ and give an account of what we believe from within His word of truth (the Bible) and not from anything outside at all (history, manuscripts, texts, language). Christian, is there no single Bible which He considers perfect? Does your Bible contain mistakes, such as bad translations? Did God tell you this? Where in the Bible has He told you this?

One way or another, the Holy Spirit has led you to this book. Knowing this, that *"we know not what we should pray for as we ought: but the Spirit itself maketh intercession for us (Rom. 8:26),"* we must be extremely careful we do not push away the hand of God regarding the King James Bible as He humbles this generation. Technically speaking, this issue has nothing at all to do with the King James Bible, although it is absolutely embodied in the King James Bible. Be sure, I am not writing in defense of the King James Bible. God's umbrage is not that God's people do not believe that He has finished the King James Bible. God's umbrage is that they do not believe that He has finished any Bible! According to the way of Israel, *"The ox knoweth his owner, and the ass his master's crib: but Israel doth not know, my people doth not consider (Isa. 1:3)."*

Actually, the divine matter we will discover in this book, that God finished His word in the King James Bible, has everything to do with:

- *The heart of the Father*

- *The character of the Father*

- *The perfection of the Son*

Can you honestly say that if God showed you that the King James Bible is sanctified by Him from all others, you would bear the personal outcome in your life to believe? Your willingness to believe will dramatically affect your illumination in reading this book. We are all dealing with an awesome God who is due the fear of His name, who conceals secrets and reveals secrets, therefore we must always be willing in all things or we run the risk of ending on the wrong side of divine matters.

CHAPTER 3

SATAN, THE SELF AND THE KJV

SATAN HIMSELF IS TRANSFORMED INTO
AN ANGEL OF LIGHT. THEREFORE, IT IS
NO GREAT THING IF HIS MINISTERS
ALSO BE TRANSFORMED AS THE
MINISTERS OF RIGHTEOUSNESS

2 CORINTHIANS 11:14,15

This chapter is extremely critical. Regarding Satan, the more I bear the life of Christ, the more Satan is eclipsed by the glory of God and I desire to give him only magnification as is necessary. Regarding the self, this deals heavily with the role of the destiny of a human soul. To me, this above all is not a light matter as choices in time cannot be undone in eternity.

Man's very first moral choice in time involved Satan, the self and the word of God. It is no exaggeration to say that man's eternal destiny for every human soul was hanging on Adam and Eve's careful hearing of every word which proceeded out of the mouth of God, *"Of every tree of the garden thou mayest freely eat: But of the tree of the knowledge of good and evil, thou shalt not eat of it: for in the day that thou eatest thereof thou shalt surely die (Gen. 2:16,17)."*

When Satan spoke his first words to man, his words were, *"Yea, hath God said, Ye shall not eat of every tree of the garden? (Gen. 3:1)."* Of course, when compared with the above, these words are a reversal and a subtraction of the actual word of God *"Of every tree of the garden thou mayest freely eat"* in 2:16,17 and from this we could say that the first Satanic Bible was published. Similar… but different.

Eve's response to Satan was, *"We may eat of the fruit of the trees of the garden: But of the fruit of the tree which is in the midst of the garden, God hath said, Ye shall not eat of it, neither shall ye touch it, lest ye die (Gen. 3:2,3)."* With the words *"neither shall ye touch it"* she added to the word of God and published the second counterfeit Bible. Again, similar but different.

In the short term, Satan had moved man from God's word to fall prey. In the long term a trend was in place bringing man into a partnership of complicity with Satan for the publishing of counterfeit Bibles. At this point, there was only one inspired version from God in Gen. 2:16,17 and two counterfeit versions in Gen. 3:1-3, one from Satan and one from Eve. Satan understood the tie he was forming and the scope of the deal for the future. For Eve, it was an unrecognized joint effort and remains quite hidden as such to this day in the world of Bible publishing.

In time to come, the inspired word of God would grow, and the counterfeit Bibles would stack up beside. Satan would for history long direct man to live by the tree of knowledge complicating his view and recognition of the inspired word of God. Time would not end before this campaign from the beginning would overtake the world. Conservatively speaking, the world now has 100 plus different main stream Bibles for you to choose from, all different from each other, and that is just the English language alone. An honest heart with a moderate handling of the Bible can easily find omissions, additions and conflicting meanings just like in the garden. Beyond these, is the man of knowledge who weekly from the pulpit says, "a better translation is…" rendering yet another version, time and time again. However, as in the garden, so now, there is only one inspired word of God no matter how many versions come along, as we shall see in this book.

The trend of Satan conjoined with man, from the beginning and in place still, is as follows:

1. Doubt God's word – *Yea, hath God said? (Gen. 3:1)*
2. Contradict God's word – *Ye shall not surely die (Gen. 3:4)*
3. Replace God's word – *Ye shall be as gods, knowing good and evil (Gen. 3:5)*

The Lord Jesus ratified to the church with His words in the New Testament parables that this revelation stands true regarding Satan's moving:

1. Steal God's word – *…Satan cometh immediately, and taketh away the word (Mark 4:15)*
2. Choke God's word – *…choke the word, and it becometh unfruitful (Mark 4:19)*
3. Mingle with tares – *…his enemy came and sowed tares among the wheat (Matt. 13:25)*

Take warning, Eve was blindsided by her "self" influenced by "other Bible versions." The unimportance of the Bible version issue to any individual is not an objective Bible influenced thought from the Father. In other words, you are not getting that thought from the Bible or the Father. Rather, it is a subjective thought that the "self" both interprets and projects into you as unimportant. It is your own projection in your own mind that you live in apart from God.

This is the deception of the self, thereby a spiritual issue and not one of intelligence. More "information" will not help you. Spiritual issues require revelation from the Father. The truth is you will not know the full implications of the KJV as God's actual word and finished Bible until you have come to it with your heart full of willingness and conviction to receive it as such. Just like you will not truly know who Jesus is until you are actually saved by Him.

Satan's first words were, *"Yea, hath God said…? (Gen. 3:1)."* This is a "Yes" and a "No" communication at the same time, to which Jesus says, *"But let your communication be, Yea, yea; Nay, nay: for whatsoever is more than these cometh of evil (Matt. 5:37)."* You may be communicating "Yes" out of one side of your mouth regarding the inspiration, inerrancy and preservation of the Bible while saying "No" out of the other side of your mouth since you deny any Bible that is God's perfect Bible in actuality. Like Jesus, the KJV may appear unexpectedly in your life, led by the Spirit, as an issue to be dealt with and your opportunity to believe in it in this perfect way may pass you by forever. The real Bible will escape from you concealed if you are not interested from the heart and willing at any cost to believe.

God willing, this book will help you, the Christian believer. Be a patient reader and all your many racing questions in your heart will be answered by the mighty King James Bible. Don't lose opportunity to correct your faith in this crucial matter to the Father. Choices made in time cannot be undone in eternity.

CHAPTER 4

JESUS, THE WORD OF GOD 1

AND THE WORD WAS MADE FLESH, AND DWELT AMONG US...

JOHN 1:14

The concept of 'word' is extremely deep and extremely mysterious as it belongs to the vastness of abstract thought, and abstract thought belongs to God:

In the beginning was the Word, and the Word was with God, and the Word was God (John 1:1)

In essence, a 'word' is a container for a spirit. God is one with His word because it contains His essential and exact spirit. The KJV capitalizes "Word" when making a clarification to the person of Christ as the "Word," rather than the Bible which is also the "word" but with a lower case "w." Still, a person and their words are indivisible. So, when the "Word" of God came He was the incarnation of the "word" of God:

And the Word was made flesh, and dwelt among us, (and we beheld his glory, the glory as of the only begotten of the Father,) full of grace and truth (John 1:14)

And…

No man hath seen God at any time; the only begotten Son, which is in the bosom of the Father, he hath declared him (John 1:18)

The word of God is deep within Him and no man can know it until He speaks. When the Father spoke, He spoke from His bosom. The bosom signifies where all spoken words come from, the lungs, deep within the person. The bosom also signifies the heart which runs deeper yet and is more mysterious than the lungs.

In John, when the Word was made flesh in Jesus, He was a container for the Father and was one with the Father. Though the Son was distinct from the Father, He was not separate from the Father because He was His Word containing His essential and exact spirit. The Father was abiding in the Son (John 14:10,11). Those who do not believe the deity of Christ have made a tragic under sight.

The above truth is so mysterious that if you would have lived in Jesus' day, you would have looked at him… walked right past Him… and thought "nothing special" and then you would have just gone on with your life.

We have another very deep and mysterious item… the Bible. This too, like Jesus, is the embodiment of God in word. Maybe you do not see the Bible to be so mysterious. This means Jesus is not mysterious to you. This means you see Jesus and the Bible as a set of facts. To you, Jesus is doctrinal facts and not a mysterious person who lives inside of your spirit. Likewise, the Bible is a doctrinal encyclopedia to you, and not a mysterious oracle that lives in you. Jesus is a figurine and the Bible is a hand book.

Because the Bible is the word of God containing His essential and exact spirit in word, it is also the embodiment of the Son and the Son is the embodiment of the word. This is why the King James Bible says what other Bibles omit:

For there are three that bear record in heaven, the Father, the Word, and the Holy Ghost: and these three are one (1 John 5:7)

Jesus, the Word of God, bears record and the Bible is that record: a book is for recording. 1 John 5:7 sources from Deuteronomy 30:19, 20 where we have confirmation that *"the Word (1 John 5:7)"* is *"his voice (Deut. 30:20)"* and His voice is both the scriptures and the Son.

We can say, in some unexplainable way to us, that the Bible is a book that turned into a person and that Jesus is a person who turned into a book, and all this without severing union each from the other. Since we have nothing to compare this reality to, we are relegated to faith, which through abstract thinking, can apprehend the truth without the necessity of comprehending the truth. This means we can apprehend, or taste and lay hold of the vision with the heart for its splendidness, while not comprehending how this can be so. Such is the vastness of the abstract thinking of God, which without, we cannot as much as begin knowing Him.

Man is desperate for this revelation. In his desperation he will spend millions of dollars to write a script and turn the script into live characters who embody the writing. All this only to produce a broken version on film to feed man's hunger for that which is beyond him and can only be fulfilled in the super naturalness of the truth. No book will ever become a man and no man will ever become a book out of Adam kind, but will always essentially remain separate from each other, and one will be the imitation and the limitation of the other.

Today, millions and millions of people live in the day of the published King James Bible. They look at it… walk right past it… and think "nothing special" about it, and then go on with their Christian life. This too is a tragic under sight.

The deep and mysterious oneness of Jesus and the Bible will be continued in the next chapters of this book and will conclude in presenting His authentic dwelling in the scriptures known to us as the King James Bible, concealed from the wise and revealed to babes. Humble yourself before Jesus, the Word of God, and touch the spirit of this word:

At that time Jesus answered and said, I thank thee, O Father, Lord of heaven and earth, because thou hast hid these things from the wise and prudent, and hast revealed them unto babes. Even so, Father: for so it seemed good in thy sight (Matt. 11:25,26)

CHAPTER 5

JESUS, THE WORD OF GOD 2

That Which Was From The Beginning, Which We Have Heard, Which We Have Seen With Our Eyes, Which We Have Looked Upon, And Our Hands Have Handled, Of The Word Of Life

1 JOHN 1:1

The mystery that the Word has come to us from the bosom of the Father in Jesus is the epitome of the Father and the Son's oneness (John 10:30; 14:9). In Colossians, the revelation is spelled out to us this way, *"Who is the image of the invisible God… (1:15)."* Every word is also an image, particularly when it is in written form as in the case of the Bible. Like the abstract thinking required for "Word", we must ponder "image".

This revelation of Jesus as *"the image of the invisible God"* speaks of a drawing out the one from the other. There is an essential oneness whether this "Word image" is concealed in God or revealed to the world. This would be true of the Bible too, which is also God's "word image".

To be "drawn out" is different than to be "drawn of". To be drawn out means the one has its nature in the other and has come forth. This is likened to the setting of the sun over the ocean. We see the sun in the sky and we see the image of the sun reflecting on the face of the deep. This image is drawn out from the original source. Contra wise, to be drawn of means one is an image of the other by a secondary source. In this case we may see the sun over the ocean and a painting of the sun over the ocean. The one is drawn of the other but there is no living relationship between the two.

So, by way of the first example in contrast to the second example, we better grasp the living relationship of the Father and the Son. The Son is drawn out of the Father and therefore is one with the Father in actuality while yet preserving distinction. Everything that is true of the Father is true of the Son. For example: The Father is God, and Jesus is God (Isa. 45:5/John 10:33); the Father gives men to Christ, and Jesus draws men to Himself (John 6:65/John 12:32); the Father raised Jesus from the dead, and Jesus raised Himself from the dead (Acts 10:40/John 10:18); the Father indwells the sons of God, and Jesus indwells the sons of God (Eph. 4:6/John 17:26). This is a partial list of an expanse.

In this same way Jesus is one with the Bible. Am I talking about Jesus or am I talking about the Bible? Study the following verses:

- *The Bible cannot be broken, and Jesus' bones cannot be broken (Ps. 34:20/ John 10:35)*

- *The Bible is the truth, and Jesus is the truth (John 17:17/John 14:6)*

- *The Bible is in God's right hand, and Jesus is seated at God's right hand (Rev. 5:1/Heb. 10:12)*

- *The Bible discerns the heart, and Jesus discerns the heart (Heb. 4:12/ Matt. 9:4)*

- *The Bible is life, and Jesus is life (Phil. 2:16/1 John 5:12)*

- *The Bible is the living bread, and Jesus is the living bread (Matt. 4:4/ John 6:51)*

- The Bible is light, and Jesus is light (Ps. 119:105/John 8:12)

- The Bible is for stumbling, and Jesus is for stumbling (1 Pet. 2:8/Rom. 9:33)

- The Bible to make joy full, and Jesus to make joy full (1 John 1:4/John 15:11)

- The word of God abides in you, and Jesus abides in you (1 John 2:14/Phil. 4:13)

- The Bible is eaten, and Jesus is eaten (Jer. 15:16/John 6:57)

- The Bible is forever settled, and Jesus is forever settled (Ps. 119:89/Rev. 22:13)

- The Bible abides forever, and Jesus abides forever (1 Pet. 1:23/John 12:34)

- The Bible is pure, and Jesus is pure (Prov. 30:5/1 John 3:3)

- The Bible is sought after, and Jesus is sought after (Isa. 34:16/Matt. 28:5)

- The Bible is to be heard and obeyed, and Jesus is to be heard and obeyed (James 1:22/Matt. 7:24)

- The Bible is incorruptible, and Jesus is incorruptible (1 Pet. 1:23/Acts 2:27)

- The Bible dwells in your heart, and Jesus dwells in your heart (Col. 3:16/Eph. 3:17)

- The Bible is always with us, and Jesus is always with us (Ps. 119:98/Matt. 28:20)

- The Bible cannot be hidden from, and Jesus cannot be hidden from (Heb. 4:12/Heb. 4:13)

- *The Bible sanctifies, and Jesus sanctifies (John 17:17/John 17:19)*

- *The Bible for everlasting life, and Jesus for everlasting life (Acts 13:46/John 3:16)*

- *The Bible is called faithful and true, and Jesus is called Faithful and True (Rev. 22:6/Rev. 19:11)*

This last one to be listed is of particular importance to the topic of this book:

- *The Bible is above God's name, and Jesus is above God's name (Ps. 138:2/Phil. 2:10)*

This too, is a partial list of an expanse. Again, am I talking about Jesus or am I talking about the Bible? I am putting before you that they are one!

Regarding the Father and the Son, and regarding the "Word" and the "word," there is both a distinction and a oneness to be equally upheld. Again, Jesus, the Word of God, and the Bible, the word of God, are distinct but are also one. We are just beginning to see we cannot accept any and every book claiming to be the "Holy Bible." Instead, we must know the actual one drawn out of the Father.

The Apostle John is captivated with Jesus as the Word of God. In 1 John 1:1 which heads this chapter, he writes that he has *"handled"* the *"Word"* in the literal sense with his *"hands."* Jesus is the embodiment of the word of God in full. The Bible is also the embodiment of the word of God in full. Therefore, in some high strangeness, John handled the finished Bible before we did because he touched Jesus with his hands. John did not know the Father's plans for the elaborate developing of the twenty first century written Bible that would end up in our hands, as we will see in chapters ahead, so he was not conscience of this touching the "Bible" as we know it, in this unique way. Truly, the deep and mysterious oneness of Jesus and the Bible is of the depth of the kind of Jesus and His oneness with the Father, and this is beyond our understanding but revealed for us to see. The words of this chapter serve but do not suffice.

CHAPTER 6

JESUS, THE WORD OF GOD 3

AND HE WAS CLOTHED WITH A VESTURE DIPPED IN BLOOD: AND HIS NAME IS CALLED THE WORD OF GOD

REVELATION 19:13

The above verse is describing the conclusive return of Jesus Christ. It will be extremely violent, and not without reason. We have the juxtaposition of the world and the "Word" of God. As we have already learned, this also means, by twofold-ness, the world is juxtaposed with the "word" of God. The world has held the "Word of God" and the "word of God" in contempt, in mishandling, in misrepresentation, in misidentification, in neglect, and now the end has come.

With Jesus, the Word of God, and the Bible, the word of God, is the pinnacle of the twofold-ness of the Father that "I" am to believe on. Since these two are one, the Jesus I believe in, and "I", are one, and the Bible I read, and "I", are one. Both must be upheld with the utmost of accuracy.

Those who are not seeking to sheer their heart to know God in truth but seek Him for ulterior motives, will not come into this vividly because it will remain concealed by God. In this aspect, they will be one of the five foolish virgins and not one of the five wise virgins in Jesus' parable (Matt. 25:1). This parable itself represents a twofold-ness given of God.

The twofold-ness of God is presented early to man to instruct him not to miss this way regarding the Father. Man was created an inner man and an outer man. He was created with a left side and a right side. He was also created with a top half and a bottom half. Finally, he was created male and female. If man neglects either half of either of these, he will suffer, not giving attention to what God has done.

When a man begins to seek the twofold-ness of Jesus and the Bible, he is awakened to another twofold-ness: objective and subjective reality. He hears Jesus say objectively, *"Except a man be born again, he cannot see the kingdom of God (John 3:3)."* If he does not grasp the twofold-ness of God and also lay hold of what Jesus says subjectively, *"Ye must be born again (3:6)"* he is imbalanced. He must uphold both the objective that *"a man"* must be born again and therefore the subjective *"Ye"* must be born again, or his way with God ends. Of course, this begets another twofold-ness to be upheld because once he "believes" that he must be born again he must also "possess" this new birth. Inaccuracy in half is the destruction of the whole.

When a man initially comes to Christ he has already begun embracing many of the twofold revelations of God. He comes to know: that God is one Lord in three persons; that God is immaterial in the Father and material in the Son; that he must worship in spirit and in truth; that he needs the Old Testament scriptures and the New Testament scriptures; that he needs faith and charity, faith and works, faith and patience; that he needs prayer and the word. If he does not carefully uphold the twofold-ness of either of these, there will be a tremendous down fall sooner or later. For example, faith without charity, he is nothing (1 Cor. 13:2). Faith without works, he is dead (James 2:22). And, faith without patience, he shall not inherit the promises of God (Heb. 6:12).

Since the above examples of twofold-ness can be perceived without awareness, it little dawns on him that while striving to ensure his accuracy in the person of Jesus, the Word of God, that God also requires accuracy regarding the Bible, the word of God. This is because the Bible embodies Jesus, as the issue of the Father, and the raising of the Spirit. This now also becomes another example of twofold-ness regarding the "Holy Spirit" and the "Holy Bible." This title "Holy Bible" embosses every version in every language despite countless contradictions, subtractions and additions, between each other. The first word "Holy" as in "Holy Spirit" and "Holy Bible," means set apart unto God as sanctified from all others and from all that is common. Do you believe this condition of blended Bible versions with forked communication is the work of the Holy Spirit? *"For God is not the author of confusion, but of peace, as in all churches of the saints (1 Cor. 14:33)."* Are they all "Holy" Bibles issuing from the "Holy" Spirit?

The man who takes to heart the seriousness of this twofold-ness of the Father in both the "Word" and the "word," is the same man who wants the Father's honor. As stated in the chapter, "If Any Man Will," to believe God and uphold the Bible He has issued as Holy will cost you:

> *How can ye believe, which receive honour one of another, and seek not the honour that cometh from God only? (John 5:44)*

This verse from John chapter 5 is where we see the Jews failed the twofold-ness of the Father. In half, they held the true Bible (vs. 39). In half, they would not come to the true Christ (vs. 40). To them inaccuracy in half was the destruction of the whole (vs. 45). Jesus did not want them to forsake the true scriptures for Him but to receive and uphold "both" according to the love of the Father (vs. 42, 46). In similarity, Jesus scorned the scribes and Pharisees because they would *"pay tithe"* but *"omitted the weightier matters."* Jesus corrected them, *"...these ought ye to have done, and not to leave the other undone (Matt. 23:23)."*

The matter of the true Bible sourced from God and manifested in our day puts us on the opposite end of the spectrum from the Jews regarding the twofold-ness of Jesus and the Bible. They treasured the true Bible but rejected the true Christ. We may come to the true Christ and reject the true Bible. The Father has waited long for you to come to this epiphany of His twofold-ness and to seek out the true Bible as you seek out the true Christ, that you may believe on both for God's sake: *"But without faith it is impossible to please him: for he that cometh to God must believe that he is, and that he is a rewarder of them that diligently seek him (Heb. 11:6)."*

CHAPTER 7

JESUS AND THE NATURE OF THE BIBLE 1

AND GOD SAID, LET THE EARTH BRING FORTH GRASS, THE HERB YIELDING FRUIT AFTER HIS KIND, WHOSE SEED IS IN ITSELF, UPON THE EARTH: AND IT WAS SO

GENESIS 1:11

Of course, we quite easily understand that Jesus is living. However, it is not as easy to understand that the Bible is living... but it is, *"For the word of God is quick... (Heb. 4:12)."* Likewise, it is easier to understand when we say that Jesus is the embodiment of the Bible, and it is more difficult to understand when we say that the Bible is the embodiment of Jesus.

The above Hebrews 4:12 verse continues like this, *"For the word of God is quick, and powerful, and sharper than any twoedged sword, piercing even to the dividing asunder of soul and spirit, and of the joints and marrow, and is a discerner of the thoughts and intents of the heart. Neither is there any creature that is not manifest in his sight: but all things are naked and opened unto the eyes of him with who we have to do (vs. 12-13)."* Note how this begins with *"the word of God"* and lapses into *"his sight"* and *"the eyes of him."* How is the word of God living? Jesus dwells within.

Up to this point and as we go on, do not be carnally minded and deduce that what is being said is that Jesus is the paper and the ink of the King James Bible. Allow God to show your spirit regarding all things "living."

God is the glorious author of all that is living. If it is living, it bears the glorious twofold-ness of God's authorship, which is: It is created by Him from nothing on the one hand; it possesses seed within itself to draw out further living ones of its kind on the other hand.

All that is living, inanimate and animate, bears this life trademark of the author. *"The grass"* and *"the herb (Gen. 1:11)"* are examples of this amongst the inanimate. The sun and the moon are also inanimate but not living. They are only operational and energetic but do not possess life. Above the grass and herb is the animals and the like. They are animate and bear the trademark. Minimally speaking, one must share in the high quality of the living to qualify for the trademark of God.

High above these is mankind, and higher yet is the angelic race. They both were created living and have the seed of life within them. These levels are closer in quality to the life of God Himself thereby carrying higher definition than other life forms. For example, the grass and the herb can spread their seed anywhere. The animals also, by and large, will spread their seed to many. But mankind is to take only one female and bring forth the living. The angelic race, though possessing seed within themselves, is not to take at all but is to refrain from reproducing the living. However, they broke from their defined living (Gen. 3:15; 6:2,4; Jude 6). All the living, are trademarked, licensed and copy righted by the author, granting Him all exclusive rights and privileges of ownership.

There is yet higher among the living. This would be Jesus and the Bible which are the super natural. They are living *"whose seed is in itself (Gen. 1:11)."* The grass and the herb, the animals, mankind and the angelic race must all draw out further living ones through natural and physical interaction, depositing their seed. Jesus and the bible are spirit and bring forth living ones *"after his kind (1:11)"* through a spiritual osmosis (John 3:8). This is a very, very high order of life.

Next, anything bearing this trademark is under the law of life. This law of life enacts that all living things after the original will come as a seed, grow in likeness of its source, and mature into an advanced version of itself. All living things are bound by this course. For example, a baby will naturally come a seed, grow into a youth in the likeness of its parents, and mature into advanced manhood. This cannot be stopped because it is abiding under the law of life.

This law of life is so strong that nothing short of a death blow can stop this process of seed, growth and maturity (Rom. 8:2). In the case of the super natural, Jesus and the Bible, even death cannot stop this process but actually furthers it. Jesus is living, and the word of God is living, and are abiding under the law of life according to God as we shall further see.

CHAPTER 8

JESUS AND THE NATURE OF THE BIBLE 2

Thine Eyes Did See My Substance, Yet Being Unperfect; And In Thy Book All My Members Were Written, Which In Continuance Were Fashioned, When As Yet There Was None Of Them

PSALM 139:16

Jesus and the Bible are eternal, and they are divine. *"Jesus said unto them, Verily, verily, I say unto you, Before Abraham was, I am (John 8:58)."* In the case of the Bible, it is written, *"For ever, O Lord, thy word is settled in heaven (Ps. 119:89)."*

Despite this eternal nature and despite the uncreated-ness of the divine, there is a component to each that began and was created. There came in time when Christ Jesus was made in the likeness of men and in fashion as a man, *"For unto us a child is born... (Isa. 9:6)."* Accompanying, there came in time when the word of God became a book to dwell within pages, *"Seek ye out the book of the Lord... (Isa. 34:16)."*

They both came from above on the one hand, and in taking on the form of creation they came through men on the other hand. In the way of joining creation, Jesus had need to come out of the Messianic line and the Bible had need to come out of the line of holy prophets and apostles (Ephes. 3:3-5). This placed each as a next generation and therefore under the second half of the twofold-ness of the law of the living, that being, to have their start as a seed (see previous chapter).

Regarding Jesus as a seed:

Hath not the scripture said, That Christ cometh of the seed of David...? (John 7:42)

And...

Now to Abraham and his seed were the promises made. He saith not, And to seeds, as of many, but as of one, And to thy seed, which is Christ (Gal.3:16)

Regarding the Bible as a seed:

Now the parable is this: The seed is the word of God (Luke 8:11)

And...

Being born again, not of corruptible seed, but of incorruptible, by the word of God, which liveth and abideth forever (1 Peter 1:23)

Many, many more scriptures testify to the above. This all important "seed" stage is what is called "conception" in the case of Jesus (Luke 1:31) and "inspiration" in the case of the Bible (2 Tim. 3:16).

When God creates out of seed it is marvelous! The marvel is this: the mature is already present and highly detailed and developed in the seed and will manifest without fail in due season because it is under the law of life (see previous chapter).

Begin pondering this and how it applies to the King James Bible which was destined to come, the very word of God.

CHAPTER 9

JESUS AND THE NATURE OF THE BIBLE 3

FOR THE VISION IS YET FOR AN APPOINTED TIME, BUT AT THE END IT SHALL SPEAK, AND NOT LIE: THOUGH IT TARRY, WAIT FOR IT; BECAUSE IT WILL SURELY COME, IT WILL NOT TARRY

HABAKKUK 2:3

When God finally named the first book of the Bible, He chose the name GENESIS. The first five letters of the word GENESIS spell the word GENES. Do not think this is accidental English word play. We will not finish this book without seeing that English would be the Bible's mature destiny.

Genesis contains all the seeds of the Bible. Anything that appears from cover to cover can be found originally in seed form in this all intuitive first book. As content, subjects, people, stories, doctrine, prophecy, revelation and all truth appear from Exodus to Revelation they are the manifestation of their seed in Genesis. Together they would grow into a mature Bible version.

Out of seed comes the growth of a line. The line itself is the growth and this growth is the manifestation. The growth, the line and the manifestation are the outworking of the seed which contains the maturity in its fullness, concealed by God. All of this takes place under the law of life. Nothing new that is not contained already in the seed can enter this path of destiny without artificial insemination.

Actually, in both cases, when Jesus came a seed and when the Bible came a seed, they came through artificial insemination. They had to. No righteous savior would ever come out of Adam and no holy Bible would come from the heart of sinners. To use the word "artificial" is not wrong as it is not being used in its negative definition but in its definition meaning "without regard to the particular needs of the natural course; imposed rather."

In the case of Jesus, He was artificially inseminated into the virgin Mary as a seed when the Holy Ghost had come upon her (Luke 1:35). The living Mary possessed the seed of death and therefore it was necessary that the seed of life in Jesus over ride current humanity and deliver salvation. This artificial insemination was advanced beyond our understanding because it was performed by the Highest (Luke 1:35). For example, Jesus joined humanity through Mary, but Jesus did not have Mary's blood. Would you dare to say that in Jesus' dying on the cross for your sins, Mary's blood was shed for you? Certainly, this is not the case.

When a man has the word of God in him, this too is an artificial insemination. Man is after the flesh. Man is carnally minded. Man is death. Man is enmity against God. Man cannot please God. Like Jesus, the seed of the Bible joins the heart by artificial insemination and comes out of the mouth, by the Holy Ghost and the Lord (Deut. 18:18; Isa. 51:16; 59:21; Jer. 1:9; Luke 12:12; Rom. 10:9,10; 2 Cor. 4:13; 2 Pet. 1:21). This too is necessary that the word of life could over rule death and deliver the salvation of the Lord. This too is a highly complex work of the Lord because the word of God that comes forth from each man has an attribute of his humanity. This happens without sacrificing that what is formed and comes forth is the pure word of God Himself.

After the seed stage but before the maturity stage comes a very long period of growth time. Jesus and the Bible took a very long time to grow but God went out of His way to include a glimpse of this fact. He gives us enough of an excerpt to emphasize each one's line of growth and manifestation of seed due to the law of life they were each under.

Regarding Jesus in growth:

And the child grew, and waxed strong in spirit, filled with wisdom: and the grace of God was upon him (Luke 2:40)

And...

And Jesus increased in wisdom and stature, and in favour with God and man (Luke 2:52)

Regarding the Bible in growth:

And the word of God increased (Acts 6:7)

And...

But the word of God grew and multiplied (Acts 12:24)

And...

So mightily grew the word of God and prevailed (Acts 19:20)

This glimpse is very necessary for confirming our understanding of the relationship of Jesus and the nature of the Bible. It is not fitting to the ear to hear that Jesus had less favor with God one day, but upon growth He had more favor with God another day. But that's what the above verses say from Luke. Of course, this applies to the Bible as well. So... we must ask, "what does this mean for the original scriptures and the now finished Bible regarding the favor of God?" and "does God favor the finished Bible over the writings of Moses' hand?" These are questions that God is waiting for us to ask.

CHAPTER 10

JESUS AND THE NATURE OF THE BIBLE 4

BUT WHEN THAT WHICH IS PERFECT IS COME, THEN THAT WHICH IS IN PART SHALL BE DONE AWAY

1 CORINTHIANS 13:10

We have seen that a seed is the miniature of something already perfect within it. We said that Jesus' coming a seed in Mary was of "conception by God," and the Bible's coming a seed in the prophets was of "inspiration by God."

We have seen that because a seed is already the perfect of its containment, a seed will manifest all its hidden details and concealed advancements as it grows in its line of life. For Jesus and the Bible, this growth was under the "preservation of God" so nothing could stop this, though attempts are always made.

From the time Jesus was born a seed His life was in danger: *"And when they were departed, behold, the angel of the Lord appeareth to Joseph in a dream, saying, Arise, and take the young child and his mother, and flee into Egypt, and be thou there until I bring thee word: for Herod will seek the young child to destroy him (Matt. 2:13)."* Actually, Jesus was in danger before this too. If you are familiar with the scriptures, you know that the Messianic line was often under attack in attempt to terminate the coming seed.

As he was growing, the danger continued still, *"And all they in the synagogue, when they heard these things, were filled with wrath, And rose up, and thrust him out of the city, and led him unto the brow of the hill whereon their city was built, that they might cast him down headlong. But he passing through the midst of them went his way (Luke 4:28-30)."* Despite this and more, Jesus' growth was preserved by God.

As we saw already in chapter three of this book, the Bible seed was also immediately in danger. God's word to Adam was an inspired seed, *"Of every tree of the garden thou mayest freely eat: But of the tree of the knowledge of good and evil, thou shalt not eat of it: for in the day that thou eatest thereof thou shalt surely die (Gen. 2:16,17)."* When Satan doubted, reversed and subtracted His word, this was an attack on the seed, *"Yea, hath God said, Ye shall not eat of every tree of the garden? (Gen. 3:1)."* When Eve added to God's word, so she attacked the seed also, *"We may eat of the fruit of the trees of the garden: But of the fruit of the tree which is in the midst of the garden, God hath said, Ye shall not eat of it, neither shall ye touch it, lest ye die (Gen. 3:2,3)."* Because today we can turn in our Bibles and clearly read this inspired word of God in Gen. 2:16,17, despite the attacks of Satan and Eve, we know it was a seed kept under His preservation. Fearfully consider this also, He preserved Satan and Eve's counterfeit words as well instead of removing them. Neither is it God's will to remove counterfeit Bibles today but instead to preserve you from them as you grow. I do not believe that Eve went back to Satan's version of the Bible in Gen. 3 after she grew through her experience of the sting of death (Gen. 3:13).

The growth of the Bible also remained in danger many times after this. One example was in the day of Jeremiah the prophet when he wrote of judgment to Jehoiakim king of Judah, by the word of the Lord. When it was read to the king by his servant, this happened, *"And it came to pass, that when Jehudi had read three or four leaves, he cut it with the penknife, and cast it into the fire that was on the hearth, until all the roll was consumed in the fire that was on the hearth (Jer. 36:23)."*

But what Jeremiah wrote was the word of God, therefore God said, *"Take thee again another roll, and write in it all the former words that were in the first roll, which Jehoiakim the king of Judah hath burned (vs. 28)."*

Furthermore, the attack only caused this seed to grow because it was under the preservation, *"Then took Jeremiah another scroll, and gave it to Baruch the scribe, the son of Neriah; who wrote therein from the mouth of Jeremiah all the words of the book which Jehoiakim king of Judah burned in the fire: and there were added besides unto them many like words (vs. 32)."* We can read what was preserved and its growth in many chapters of Jeremiah today.

In this time of growth, many awkward shapes occur. This is just like when children grow, their bodies take odd shape as their line of life passes through many curious stages before blossoming into maturity. When Jesus was only a child he demonstrated growth and astonished all with His understanding and answers (Luke 2:47). When Jesus was baptized by John this was a very awkward stage to him (Matt. 3:14). Then Jesus was tried by the Devil for a long suffering 40 days and 40 nights without food. This was a great growth spurt. After this, even the neighbors thought oddly of Him seeing the miracles, signs and wonders which now came forth of Him (Luke 4:22). When He came a seed, He *"was made flesh (John 1:14)"* then He grew unrecognizably until He matured and *"was made a quickening spirit (1 Cor. 15:45)"* by resurrection. Actually, everything prior to His resurrection was still growth.

We can say from another perspective that the line of growth is also a line of shedding. It is a line of shedding because the steady growth emerges and the old passes away. Do you remember when Jesus shed Mary (John 2:4)? The word of God has also gone through much awkward growth on its way to maturity and much shedding also:

> *...All flesh is grass, and all the goodliness thereof is as the flower of the field: The grass withereth, the flower fadeth: because the spirit of the Lord bloweth*

upon it: surely the people is grass. The grass wihtereth, the flower fadeth: but the word of our God shall stand for ever (Isa. 40:6-8)

The above verse says, *"All flesh is grass."* This is what the letters of the Bible were written on: Skins for the Old Testament (flesh); and papyri for the New Testament (grass). God also says that He will wear out these materials, *"because the spirit of the Lord bloweth upon it."* This means He will destroy them.

God's word "itself" though, would *"stand forever"* because it would mature. His word, which is contained as spirit within the letters of ink on the skins and papyri would be preserved and manifest forward in the growth of the line of life all the way to the finished Bible. Because it is not God's intention to keep the originals of the Bible, which were of temporary nature, anyone who tells you they are going back to the originals is a liar because God's Spirit has done away with the originals. No one has the originals. Do not put more importance on the originals than God does. This is a self-evident mistake.

Peter discerned this and said of Isaiah the prophet's words:

Being born again, not of corruptible seed, but of incorruptible, by the word of God, which liveth and abideth forever. For all flesh is grass… but the word of the Lord endureth forever… (1 Peter 1:23-25)

His "Word," Jesus, and His "word," the Bible, would shed much and transform shape a lot on the long way to maturity in the King James Bible, but they would not suffer corruption. We will talk more about this in the chapters ahead.

CHAPTER 11

JESUS AND THE NATURE OF THE BIBLE 5

> SO SHALL MY WORD BE THAT GOETH FORTH OUT OF MY MOUTH: IT SHALL NOT RETURN UNTO ME VOID, BUT IT SHALL ACCOMPLISH THAT WHICH I PLEASE, AND IT SHALL PROSPER IN THE THING WHERETO I SENT IT
>
> ISAIAH 55:11

How many times have you heard unbelievers say that the Bible is full of mistakes because, "Men wrote the Bible!"? Of course, this is folly and shame.

If we have the illumination of the Holy Spirit, we are clear that no part of the Bible was ever originally: sourced out of a man; grown by the keeping of a man; or matured by the power of a man. All of these regarding the Bible are sourcing organically and systemically according to life, by God, and not by man. God's ways and thoughts pertaining to the seed, growth and maturity of the Bible in the KJV are higher than man's, even as the heavens are higher than the earth.

When Christians say, "We believe in the verbal inspiration of the scriptures without mistakes as far as in the original writings" and the like, they are speaking with dissimilation. This is because at the same time they are speaking rich of the Bible regarding inspiration, they are also speaking poverty of the Bible by saying inspiration only pertains to its originals. Therefore, they are saying to the unbelievers that their contemporary Bible is not inspired and contains mistakes. They are also saying it is not the original, and therefore has not been kept by God in verbatim. In this way, they are trying to win unbelievers to the veracity of the Bible, as the very word of God, while at the same time creating doubt and uncertainty. This too is folly and shame.

Christians hide all the time behind the shadows of "the originals," which no longer exist when declaring inspiration and inerrancy of the Bible. They have to, because, they are not able to point to a specific Bible today and declare it God's perfect word.

Do not err, my beloved brethren. Every good and perfect gift is from above, and cometh down from the Father of lights, with whom is no variableness, neither shadow of turning (James 1:16,17)

God's Bible is of the greatest of gifts that has come down *"from above, from the Father,"* and is wholly *"perfect,"* unlike the double talk of men. "The Bible is inspired by God, but only in the originals" is the double talk of men. "The Bible is inerrant, but only in the originals" is more of the double talk of men. The next verse of the passage above states that this God *"with whom is no variableness, neither shadow of turning"* has begotten His born-again ones through *"the word of truth (vs. 18)."* Therefore, we should understand this passage as pertaining to the Bible by all means.

In fact, let's consider this question: In what verse of the Bible is God telling anyone that His word is no longer inspired or contains mistakes?

All scripture is given by inspiration of God, and is profitable for doctrine, for reproof, for correction, for instruction in righteousness: That the man of God may be perfect... (2 Tim. 3:16,17)

The above passage uses the specific present tense verb *"is,"* which strictly communicates "current" and "continuous" terms of condition. The end result is that His *"profitable scripture"* renders *"the man of God perfect"* because it is *"by inspiration of God"* and therefore without mistake itself. The scripture that Paul is referring to here when writing to Timothy is not the originals but the preserved growth of the originals in his time. Please know that inspiration without preservation is absolutely meaningless. If what Timothy grew up on was the inspired scriptures in his day, this begs the question as to where is the inspired Bible in our day?

Let's listen to God again as He ensures us of this truth, that His living word is not stuck in time:

> *The words of the Lord are pure words: as silver tried in a furnace of earth, purified seven times. Thou shalt keep them, O Lord, thou shalt preserve them from this generation for ever (Psalm 12:6,7)*

This word is very telling. Again, we have the present tense verb, *"are,"* used. *"The words of the Lord are pure words"* actually refers to the inspired seed state in which the perfect is contained. Next, *"purified seven times"* refers to the growth state. Finally, *"thou shalt preserve them from this generation for ever"* emphasizes the overarching preservation of God from the seed state, through the growth state into the maturity state. We are between *"this generation"* and *"for ever"* which means there is a *"pure"* Bible today.

Of course, by the Bible being *"purified,"* it is not meant that it has moral deficiencies, or errors. God is speaking strictly of the unique manifestation of growth which is emerging through transformation of the maturity of life which is hidden in the seed. The inspiration is not lost at any time during this outworking but merely refined in its visible expression. This is the meaning of purification as pertaining to the things of God.

This means the growth still possesses the original. For example, if we have a grown man we cannot say he is not the original child. Even though he has outgrown the child, still the original child is present within him. This is an accurate understanding of the matter and this is how we must understand the inspiration and preservation of the living Bible.

The opposite is also true, and we have hinted at it. Even as the growth actually has the original in it, so the original has the growth in it and even the mature. This line of life is a course just as is described in our chapter heading verse:

So shall my words be that goeth forth out of my mouth: it shall not return unto me void, but it shall accomplish that which I please, and it shall prosper in the thing whereto I sent it (Isa. 55:11)

God's words which *"goeth forth"* are seeds. Because they contain the mature edition within, God says, *"they will not return unto me void,"* which means empty. To return empty to Him would require the loss of inspiration along the way. This is not the case because they are preserved, so they will grow and *"accomplish"* all that God pleases. Remember two chapters ago that the Father was pleased all the more as Jesus grew (Luke 2:40,52)? As God's words grow they are maturing and coming into their prosperity. At this mature stage they will accomplish even more than when they were in seed form. This is the condition in which they will *"return unto"* Him after completing their course in the world. This is a circuit from the Father, into the world and back to the Father.

We see again in the next verse below, that the words of God returned to Him mature. They began the circuit in His mouth but returned into His right hand. His right hand signifies maturity because His right hand is His strength. This is from Revelation, the last book in the Bible:

And I saw in the right hand of him that sat on the throne a book written within and on the backside, sealed with seven seals (5:1)

This is the matured Bible in God's hand which returned to Him in the end according to His Isaiah 55:11 declaration. You may say that you do not believe that this book in the Father's hand is the Bible as indeed the Father has many books. I assure you that there is only one book that will be presented to us in the Father's right hand even as Jesus is at the Father's right hand, and this book is the Bible.

The Apostle John saw this perfect Bible in heaven that was manifesting on earth through seed, growth and maturity. It had seven seals that no man could open. Jesus took the book out of the Father's hand to open it as He is the only one who can open it (Rev. 5:5,7). Jesus is the only one who can open any of the Bible to a man, or reveal to you that the Father's word is finished in the King James Bible:

Then opened he their understanding, that they might understand the scriptures (Luke 24:45)

This verse is from the road to Emmaus episode, where the disciples were confused about the scriptures and Jesus' apparent end at the cross. Jesus returned to them on the day He rose from the dead to ensure them He was not stuck in time but perfected, or, was of the matured version of the same Jesus they originally knew. He revealed this to them by the scriptures, the Bible.

This is the same thing that took place regarding the sealed Bible in the Father's hand in Revelation chapter five. This Bible in His hand is perfect. God only seals that which is perfect. The Bible had run its course in the world and was mature in the Father's hand. Again, we say, it requires Jesus to open the contents. At the very same time John was experiencing this regarding the sealed Bible in heaven, the Bible was growing and maturing on earth. Jesus opened the sealed Bible and John wrote it down for us in Revelation 6 and forward.

Jesus Himself also ran the course from seed, growth to maturity in the same way as the Bible:

I came forth from the Father, and am come into the world: again, I leave the world, and go forth to the Father (John 16:28)

In the Revelation chapter five appearing of the Bible in the Father's right hand, we see Jesus at the Father's right hand as well, because they are one in all things. Again, neither Jesus, the Word of God, or the Bible, the word of God, are stuck in time suffering a diminished quality. To the contrary, the truth is exactly the opposite, and both have reached the Father matured.

CHAPTER 12

Jesus And The Nature Of The Bible 6

I have also spoken by the prophets, and I have multiplied visions, and used similitudes, by the ministry of the prophets

Hosea 12:10

There is much about Jesus you and I do not understand. However, would you dare say, "He is not perfect" because you don't understand? Don't make this mistake with the perfect word of God in the King James Bible.

By now, hopefully, you are realizing that there is also much about the Bible you do not understand. Did you know it came as an inspired seed? Did you know it bears the trademark of God? Did you know it grew in the line of life? Did you know it matured to reveal what was in the seed all along? Did you know that through preservation of the seed, the mature version would contain the original inspiration? Did you know that all of this was destined to manifest without mistake because of the law of life that every seed grows after its kind and matures? Let's consider further this maturity…

Regarding Jesus' maturity, it is written:

And he said unto them, Go ye, and tell that fox, Behold, I cast out devils, and I do cures to day and to morrow, and the third day I shall be perfected (Luke 13:32)

And...

Though he were a Son, yet learned he obedience by the things which he suffered: And being made perfect, he became the author of eternal salvation unto all them that obey him (Heb. 5:8,9)

In the Luke 13:32 verse, Jesus expressed that His maturing required being resurrected as He gave King Herod the similitude of the prophets of *"the third day."*

In the Hebrews 5:8,9 passage it is also expressed that His maturing required resurrection since after *"he suffered"* He was *"made perfect."*

Regarding the Bible's maturity, it is written:

Whereof I am made a minister, according to the dispensation of God which is given to me for you, to fulfill the word of God (Col. 1:25)

And...

For I testify unto every man that heareth the words of the prophecy of this book, If any man shall add unto these things, God shall add unto him the plagues that are written in this book: And if any man shall take away from the words of the book of this prophecy, God shall take away his part out of the book of life, and out of the holy city, and from the things which are written in this book (Rev. 22:18,19)

And...

The grace of our Lord Jesus Christ be with you all. Amen (Rev. 22:21)

In the Col. 1:25 verse, Paul has awareness that his ministry of the doctrine of the indwelling Christ, will *"fulfill the word of God."* In other words, this was the peak of the Bible's maturity as related to doctrinal content. Paul therefore understood that the Bible would have a maturity.

In the Rev. 22:18,19 passage, John's words demonstrate the finality of *"this book."* John's words are in the similitude of the prophet Moses' words, found in Deuteronomy 4:1,2. John's words are the growth of Moses' words. The Bible opens and closes with this twofold witness, so we know that John's warnings in *"this book,"* apply not only to the book of revelation, but to the finished and matured Bible as one entire book.

In Rev. 22:21, the last word of the Bible is *"Amen."* This further means that it has matured. This word itself is a seal to something finished, as at the end of a prayer. In this case the volume of the Bible is sealed, and it is matured.

So far in this chapter, the word "similitude" has come up three times. This word means an "appearance" or "image" or "shape" that becomes recognizable. When a seed appears and grows, an image begins to emerge, when it matures, it has an exact shape. But between growth and maturity must come the thrust of maturity, which is death.

Going forward in this subject, let's examine death and maturity and similitude from Psalm sixteen in the life of Jesus and the Bible:

For thou wilt not leave my soul in hell; neither wilt thou suffer thine Holy One to see corruption (Psalm 16:10)

We will see that God's *"Holy One"* refers to both Jesus and the Bible.

Psalm 16:10 grows into Acts 13:35 where the resurrection of Jesus is detailed between verses thirty to forty-one. In Acts 13:33 it says this, *"God hath fulfilled the same unto us their children, in that he hath raised up Jesus again; as it is also written in the second Psalm, Thou art my Son, this day have I begotten thee."* Jesus' death was necessary for resurrection to take place.

His resurrection was the coming forth of His maturity. Therefore, death thrust Him into maturity.

The resurrected Jesus was really nothing of the kind of the original Jesus. A new Jesus was *"begotten,"* which means a new Jesus was born. God considers maturity which emerges out of death in resurrection power to be a birth of a kind. But at the same time, this new mature Jesus who was born again in this way, contained the original Jesus deep within. This is why He still referred to Himself despite resurrection maturity as the original Jesus of Nazareth, *"And I answered, Who art thou, Lord? And he said unto me, I am Jesus of Nazareth, whom thou persecutest (Acts 22:8)."*

Psalm 16 clearly refers to Jesus. But the similitude to the Bible is very strong as well. The first words of Psalm 16 set the context of the chapter and are of the utmost of importance to our topic. These words the Psalmist cries are:

Preserve me, O God… (Psalm 16:1)

The chapter is about preservation starting in verse one. In verse ten, which we covered, the declaration is made that God will preserve His Holy One from corruption. Then in verse eleven, the ending verse, we read this:

Thou wilt shew me the path of life: in thy presence is fullness of joy; at thy right hand are pleasures for ever more (Psalm 16:11)

We know from our deep coverage of Revelation 5:1 and 7 in the last chapter, that the Bible is in the Father's right hand and Jesus is at the Father's right hand. We saw in our Psalm 16:10 verse in this chapter that Jesus would not see corruption and now we see that He matures and is the pleasure of the Father in the next verse, Psalm 16:11. This parallels that the Bible would also not see corruption but mature into the Father's pleasure. Note very well, therefore, that this verse is intentionally the number 16:11, as in the "1611 King James Bible" by similitude of the prophet, and also matching Revelation 5:1 by similitude of the Apostle. The cover of this book also has a similitude of the prophet that reveals the 1611 King James Bible. This was the year that the Bible matured practically overnight out of its long growth. These similitudes of the prophets are extremely inconvenient for turning a blind eye or playing dumb to the KJV.

But these kinds of emerging details are to be expected as growth always manifests further order and complexity of intelligent design. Though it began in Hebrew and grew in Greek it was begotten in English. However, within it remains the original identity and inspiration of the Hebrew and Greek preserved. This is the same as Jesus who began, Jesus of Nazareth, but was begotten entirely different in resurrection overnight.

This kind of communicating, as in Psalm 16, which begins with one subject but ends with another without changing content, is the way of the Spirit. When something is one with another, the Spirit often begins speaking of the one and ends speaking of the other, without clarifying transition. Here, we see the Psalmist asking to be preserved in verse one, and then we see Jesus and the Bible preserved in the right hand of the Father in verse eleven. The preservation plea of the Psalmist in the first verse is bound in the preservation and maturity of both Jesus and the Bible in the last verse, which to reiterate, emerges as preserved and matured. Another example of the Spirit's speaking this way would be in Jesus' addressing the seven churches where seven times it is announced in the beginning that Jesus is speaking but conclude that it is the Spirit who is speaking to the churches (see Revelation 2 and 3).

The maturing of the Bible has suffered much violence even as Jesus suffered much violence. Both suffered death as we shall see in an upcoming chapter. Both have now passed through violence, not to be held by corruption, and have entered into their maturity, Jesus, the Lord from heaven, and the Bible, the 1611 King James Version. Still though, men look into the past to understand what is in the present because they do not believe. They look to that which was buried and left in corruption for thousands of years, like the Dead Sea scrolls and other emerging manuscripts to put their trust in for clarifying God's word, when the living matured word of God is right in their midst. To this we can only say along with the word of God:

Why seek ye the living among the dead? (Luke 24:5)

And...

Do ye not therefore err, because ye know not the scriptures, neither the power of God? He is not the God of the dead, but the God of the living: ye therefore do greatly err (Mark 12:24, 27)

CHAPTER 13

JESUS AND THE NATURE OF THE BIBLE 7

...EVERY MAN AT THE BEGINNING DOTH SET FORTH GOOD WINE; AND WHEN MEN HAVE WELL DRUNK, THEN THAT WHICH IS WORSE: BUT THOU HAST KEPT THE GOOD WINE UNTIL NOW

JOHN 2:10

We saw in the last chapter, that the Psalmist cried *"Preserve me (Ps. 16:1),"* and that the Father answered this prayer by not allowing His *"Holy One to see corruption (Ps. 16:10)."* The Psalmist's life could only be preserved in Jesus and the Bible which are His *"Holy One,"* because they are God's single *"path of life (Ps. 16:11; Ps. 119:105; John 14:6)."*

We saw that the Psalmist's hope was indeed in the right place as he saw details, yet through a glass darkly. The details he saw through a glass darkly were that not he, but rather, Jesus and the Bible would arrive preserved unto the Father, *"at thy right hand there are pleasures forever more (Ps. 16:11)."*

We saw that in order to see this more clearly today than the Psalmist, we need Psalm sixteen to grow into John's testimony in Revelation five. There we see the pleasures of the Father's right hand, which are the maturation of the Bible and Jesus, *"And I saw in the right hand of him that sat on the throne a book... And he (Jesus) came and took the book out of the right hand of him that sat upon the throne (Rev. 5:1,7)."*

We saw that this great revelation is summed up purposely by the Spirit in Psalm 16:11, revealing the 1611 King James Bible. The Psalmist saw all this by way of vague image, as he and the revelation were both still growing in time. Today, the revelation is matured but we are still growing, so like the Psalmist, we see this by way of faint image also. This is one reason it is hard to discern the true Bible from the counterfeits.

Also, it is hard to discern the true Bible from the counterfeits because God has concealed it, for His glory. However, as we mature, despite concealment, we see the actual Jesus and the actual Bible in the 1611 King James Version, for who and what they are in their exact shape, even as the Father sees. Then we may revel with the Father in His right-hand pleasures, because our faith in Jesus and the word of God will be purified (Heb. 11:6; 1 John 3:2; John 15:8).

We also saw in the last chapter that when Jesus resurrected He was nothing like His previous version. He was a spiritual body. He walked through walls. He entered into people. We could say he was a translated version of Himself. Yet, the original inspired seed had not departed as He was still possessing Himself as Jesus of Nazareth. This super condition was His maturity. He will never change now.

The Bible has also transformed by design. We are just starting to have vision that the 1611 King James Bible is the true seed of God, and we will sharpen this as we go. It is also a translated version of the original. What began in Hebrew and Greek has matured into English by the will and preservation of God by passing through death which will be the focus of our next chapter. Here too, the inspiration is not lost, but issuing the maturity. The Bible will never change again. This is why the KJV has not been changed for "better words" or "contemporary words" for over four hundred years unlike other so-called Bibles.

Jesus and the Bible were made one way as a seed and made another way in maturity:

Thou fool, that which thou sowest is not quickened, except it die: And that which thou sowest, thou sowest not that body that shall be, but bare grain, it may chance of wheat, or of some other grain: But God giveth it a body as it hath pleased him, and to every seed a body (1 Cor. 15:36-38)

In both the raising up of Jesus and the raising up of the Bible, the Father *"giveth it a body as it hath pleased him, and to every seed a body (vs. 38)."* Therefore, we ought to expect that serious differences are to be. The most common pitfall that overtakes man, in regard to God's finished Bible, is in this area of God giving the mature word a body that pleases him. They presume that words from the Greek and Hebrew are falsely translated in the KJV. This is where men lean on their own understanding and criticize falsely. However, the author has selected the defining translation He desires, and each word has the correct English body despite that it may look nothing like the Hebrew or Greek seed. Therefore, a better translation is not to be, though men feel that they have scholastic warrant to boast so. We will devote an entire chapter to this subject onward.

For now, answer this question: is there anything that God does better in the beginning than at the end? In other words, is there anything that God begins and does not end with a superior version of?

In Genesis God creates the heaven and the earth. In Revelation God creates a new heaven and a new earth. Which is superior?

Out of the dust God makes an earth man. In Christ a man is recreated as a spirit man. Which is superior?

A man is born. A man must be born again. Which is superior?

We were given the Old Testament. We were given the New Testament. Which is superior?

The law is given to Israel. The Spirit is given to the church. Which is superior?

God works with Israel in the beginning. God works with Israel in the end. Which is superior?

Jerusalem comes first. The new Jerusalem comes at the end. Which is superior?

There was the temple of Solomon where God dwelt. There is now the temple of the body where God dwells. Which is superior?

There is the first death and there is the second death. Which is superior?

And most particular to our focus…

Jesus was made flesh. Jesus was resurrected in glory. Which is superior?

And…

The Bible was sown in Hebrew and Greek and a little Aramaic. It was matured in English. Which is superior?

Be careful how you answer the last question, especially in light of the header verse of this chapter. God is not like a man. He does not start with good and then serve worse. He does not go from superior to inferior. As He works there is a manifold arrangement of sophisticated blossom. In this way, God saves the best for last. And that which is last remains. Again, the 1611 King James Bible will never go away but will remain forever. The other false Bible versions will all be destroyed by fire in the end because they are not born of the Spirit. They are not of God's seed and they do not have the line of His life or bear His maturity. They are void of the Spirit and they are antichrist.

On this note, we are entering the most important aspect of maturity, which is the ruling and reigning of life in its members. Both Jesus and the Bible, through the maturity of the divine seed, have passed through death and have entered into this ruling and reigning in life. When Jesus was begotten through the resurrection, Satan understood that the ascension of Christ was a final matter. Jesus' fragile humanity was now galvanized into His deity and as the God-Man He would forever be exalted. Due to this final transformation of maturity, Satan would have no chance of destroying Christ as previously attempted. His strategy switched to focusing on false Christ's to deceive the world. By multiplying Christ versions and gospel versions tares would be sown among the wheat.

When the King James Bible was begotten, Satan knew again that life had wholly consumed the body of the canon and there was no way he could ever destroy the Bible. The two, Hebrew and Greek, had become one galvanized into English as God's glorified Bible and would never be changed in the 1611 King James Bible. This takes us into today, where the only attempt to destroy can be by multiplying counterfeits, which is the extreme case. As false Christs, so false Bibles. However, no matter how many counterfeits come alongside the King James Bible, it will never go away because it is wrought of the Spirit in kingdom power of life: *"For whatsoever is born of God overcometh the world (1 John 5:4)."*

It is God's only begotten Bible and there will always be a voice in the church crying out the truth to its authority. Is there any other version of the Bible that the church defends as the actual inspired word of God? This phenomenon is a warning. A part of the body of Christ feels the attack and cries out in pain to the rest of the body. But the body is forsaking the mind of Christ.

When Christians proclaim the gospel, it is far and few between who include the ascension of Jesus Christ. If they barely are in touch in their spirit with the ascension of Christ and its application in their own Christian walk, then of course there is little chance they will understand it in the role of the Holy Bible. Ascension is the high position of authority, as was pictured in Joseph who was at the right hand of Pharaoh, after his suffering, to rule and reign the world empire of his day. The one who has the life has the authority. Such also, is the King James Bible as it has gone from suffering to glory now bearing the authority of the Father's right hand. We must have eyes to see this and not try and artificially take the Bible beyond its maturity and disfigure it by rivaling translations, or we will end up with a man-made counterfeit every time.

Which Jesus do you want? The Jesus before He was perfected? Or the Jesus after He was perfected? Which Bible do you want? The original or the final perfected version?

Chapter 14

Man, The Cross, And The KJV

And From The Days Of John The Baptist Until Now The Kingdom Of Heaven Suffereth Violence, And The Violent Take It By Force

Matthew 11:12

When God finished the Bible in the King James Version, He did so at the height of English development. Though the vernacular speech of the land in 1611 was not spoken as you read it in the KJV, with words like "thus" or "sayeth" or "thy" or "thine," etc., these words were selected for scholastic purposes. They are highly intelligent words that trans-mission faithfully into English the difference between singular and plural words, as found in the original languages of the scriptures. Other sophisticated words that are used actually carry theological import as well as skillful cross referencing by divine inspiration. Not a word is wasted in the KJV.

Over all, it is a literary masterpiece. The era was that of William Shakespeare, who was in King James' service during the preparation of the Authorized Version of the Bible. As Shakespeare might have said, "The stage has been set…" God had predestinated and called King James prophetically in His word to come to the kingdom for such a time as this:

He sheweth his word unto Jacob… (Ps. 147:19)

Jacob is the Hebrew rendering of "James." In the literal text of this verse it defines Jacob as Israel, of course. And it goes into the next verse to say that God *"hath not dealt so with any nation (vs. 20),"* referring to shewing His word. However, the word of God was entrusted over to the gentiles now and the time to deal His word to them had come. "James" was seeded into *"Jacob (vs. 19)"* as the spirit of prophecy.

A divine sentence is in the lips of the king (Prov. 16:10)

This was the king's English and it demanded men look up to it. Many people say they cannot understand the King James Bible. This is a sad statement regarding their own condition, as the KJV is a mere fifth grade reading level at whole, with many parts being even lower. The claim of archaic words is also an over rated cry, especially considering the Holy Spirit built-in dictionary of the KJV. God's Holy Bible is not to be lowered to our standard: *"Study to shew thyself approved unto God, a workman that needeth not to be ashamed, rightly dividing the word of truth (2 Tim. 2:15)."* If you began an educational course would you say to the teacher, "This text book is too hard for me to understand. Can I get one that is easier?" The means and the end result of the King James Bible was to know God through looking up.

Compare the spirit of the age to just a few of the men of God:

…O, Lord; in the morning will I direct my prayer unto thee, and will <u>look up</u> (Ps.5:3)

In the year that King Uzziah died I saw also the Lord sitting upon a throne, <u>high and lifted up</u>… (Isa. 6:1)

I press toward the mark for the prize of <u>the high calling</u> of God in Christ Jesus (Phil. 1:21)

After this I looked, and, behold, a door was opened in heaven... <u>Come up</u> hither, and I will shew thee things which must be here after (Rev. 4:1)

...<u>look up</u>, and <u>lift up your heads</u>; for your redemption draweth nigh (Luke 21:28)

And I, <u>if I be lifted up</u> from the earth, will draw all men unto me (John 12:32)

God's way is for His things to be over man's head. This last verse, in particular, will take us into our chapter topic. Jesus spoke these words about His death on the cross, where Satan wanted Jesus to come down, even as he wants the Bible to come down, *"Save thyself, and come down from the cross (Mark 15:30)."*

You might think that the call to *"come down from the cross"* only applies to Jesus, but it also applies to the Bible. It too had to pass through death in order to mature in life and take its high and lifted up place at God's right hand. This death of the Bible took place with Jesus on the cross at the hands of wicked men. But how? Am I saying that Jesus, who is the Word of God, was crucified, therefore the Bible in Him as well? I am saying that, but I am also saying much, much more.

The cross is the vortex center of world history. From the beginning, the Bible and Jesus were always moving closer to this center point and to each other, until they would meet in person at the cross. All things working together, Jesus literally crossed paths with the Bible at the cross to share sufferings. It was necessary, due to their two-fold nature, that they die together in picture. And so, it was:

And Pilate wrote a title, and put it on the cross. And the writing was, JESUS OF NAZARETH THE KING OF THE JEWS... and it was written in Hebrew, and Greek, and Latin (John 19;19,20)

This key event is also recorded in Matthew and Mark and Luke's gospel record where we have additional details supplied. Together, there are three points in this move of Pilate that we need to closely glean from.

The first point is that these words, "JESUS OF NAZARETH THE KING OF THE JEWS," written by Pilate, are the word of God. Pilate's very words are inspired scripture. This is testified to by the Spirit who interprets Pilate's words using the term *"superscription,"* which includes the word *"script,"* which is the short hand of "scripture." This is pointed out in Mark 15:26, *"And the superscription of his accusation was written over, THE KING OF THE JEWS (Mark 15:26)."*

Even as the Romans did not know they had nailed Jesus, the Word of God, to the cross, so they did not know they had nailed the Bible, the word of God to the cross either. Both had been crucified. The Spirit gives a second witness to this through Paul in Colossians 2:14, *"Blotting out the handwriting of ordinances that was against us, which was contrary to us, and took it out of the way, nailing it to his cross."* The choice of the word *"blotting"* refers to the blood of Jesus. The *"handwriting of ordinances"* refers to the law given to Moses written by God's finger. This amounts to the Bible, and *"it"* was nailed to *"his cross"* when Pilate nailed the *"superscription"* to the cross.

The second point that we must see is that the *"superscription"* was written in *"Hebrew and Greek and Latin."* This was prophetically representing the plenary of the Bible which had been nailed to the cross. As the Old Testament was written in Hebrew, this was the seed of the Bible. The emerging New Testament, written in Greek, was the growth. The Latin, of course, was the seed of English, and therefore represented the maturity of the Bible as it would come to be in the King James Version. Do not despise this thought, that the English was present in the Latin. Do you not remember that likewise, it was accounted to Levi that he paid tithes to Melchisedec, before he was born, while he was but a seed in his great grandfather Abraham's body? For it is written: *"And as I may so say, Levi also, who receiveth tithes, payed tithes in Abraham (Heb. 7:9)."* This is God's way.

Some may say regarding this point that the only reason that this *"superscription"* was written in *"Hebrew and Greek and Latin"* is because these were the languages of the land, end of story. But the reader must always see spiritually beyond the letter of the Bible or he will die (2 Cor. 3:6). Do not quench the Spirit but be reminded of when the Father spoke prior, also regarding the crucifixion of Jesus: *"Father, glorify thy name. Then came there a voice from heaven, saying, I have both glorified it, and will glorify it again. The people therefore, that stood by, and heard it, said that it thundered: others said, an angel spake to him (John 12:28,29)."* Do you hear thunder or a voice from heaven?

The third point takes us back to where we began this chapter, demanding men look up to the word of God lifted high:

And set up over his head his accusation written, THIS IS JESUS THE KING OF THE JEWS (Matt. 27:37)

Jesus was aware that the Bible was over his head. As man's substitute, He knew He was intentionally placed beneath it by the hand of God. Despite the pain, His mind was on the Bible:

After this, Jesus knowing that all things were now accomplished, that the scripture might be fulfilled, saith, I thirst. Now there was set a vessel full of vinegar, and put it upon hyssop, and put it to his mouth. When Jesus therefore had received the vinegar, he said, It is finished: and he bowed his head, and gave up the ghost (John 19:28-30)

"It is finished" applies to many things including the Bible. When Jesus said those words, it was out of His knowing that *"all things were now accomplished, that the scripture might be fulfilled."* Do not think He was saying *"It is finished"* to the crowd or even looking at them. He was not performing. He was looking up to *"It,"* the Bible, above His head and saying, *"It is finished,"* speaking to the Father. This is why after these words *"he bowed his head,"* from a looking up position.

In the Spirit, Jesus knew everybody, and the role they would occupy in history and eternity. He knew Nathaniel, in whom was no guile, before He ever met him (John 1:47). And He knew Judas, in whom was guile, before He ever met him (John 6:70). In light of all we have seen, when He was dying on the cross, it is hard to believe He did not also know King James already.

CHAPTER 15

A BODY HAST THOU PREPARED ME 1

THEN SAID I, LO, I COME (IN THE VOLUME OF THE BOOK IT IS WRITTEN OF ME,) TO DO THY WILL, O GOD

HEBREWS 10:7

In the Bible, the seeds that God has planted in Genesis are growing all throughout and reaching maturity in Revelation. Even bad seeds like Satan begin in Genesis, where he comes as a serpent but grows into a dragon by the end (Rev. 20:2).

But of all of God's seeds, one is exceptional beyond the rest. This seed is the human body. It ranks as the premier seed because in the human body, Jesus, the Word of God, joins man:

...and was made in the likeness of men: And being found in fashion as a man... (Phil. 2:7,8)

Everything between God and man is bridged and fulfilled in this seed, the human body. We first see this seed as Abraham's tent wherein the Lord fellowshipped with Abraham (Gen. 18:1ff). There they shared in three of the offerings together: the drink offering (vs. 4); the meal offering (vs. 5); the sin offering (vs. 7). This was a miniature of the tabernacle and the offerings.

The seed of Abraham's tent grew in Exodus, in the time of Moses, and it became a big tabernacle. Father Abraham's tent supported a family meeting place with the Lord for the offerings but now they were a great people. This required many more offerings which had further grown by this time as well, and many more partakers meeting there, and many more priests entering in, and of course the presence of the Lord.

In the day of Solomon, this tent for the in dwelling of the Lord and a family, that grew into a tabernacle for the in dwelling of the Lord and a people, had now grown into a very large temple. This temple was now sized for the in dwelling of the Lord and a nation to fulfill all righteousness.

After this, the Word was made flesh in Jesus as the further growth of the temple. Abraham's tent was satisfactory for a family, and the wilderness tabernacle for a great people, even the temple of Solomon for a nation, but now the reconciliation of the world, that all men may enter into God, was at hand. This required the unlimited and universal Christ as the enlargement of the temple of God and the fulfillment of the offerings. The presence of God was in Christ and so were the people of God (John 14:2). The body of Jesus Christ was a bigger temple than Solomon's temple.

When Jesus was raised up from the dead, the growth of the Father's temple increased yet again (Ephes. 2:6; 1 Pet. 1:3). All who were in Christ were raised with Him and began to be born again one by one and the temple of God spread. Now there are many temples in the world all containing the fullness of Christ. Together these bodies make up the true temple of God wherein He dwells and mingles with His people in the same way He did with Abraham enjoying the offerings. If you are born again you are a part of this massive temple (1 Pet. 1:23; 2:5).

Finally, this massive temple will mature in expression in the New Jerusalem, which appears in Revelation as God and man's final and mature dwelling together, for the desire and expression of God (Rev. 21:2,3,9).

From Abraham's tent, to Moses' tabernacle, to Solomon's temple, we have the testimony of the human body, which was clearly revealed in its arrival in Jesus Christ, *"For in him dwelleth all the fullness of the Godhead bodily (Col. 2:9)"* and unto, in, the church for eternity (Ephes. 3:9; Col. 3:11).

All of this shows God's extreme claim and purpose of the human body. Therefore, we must not resist giving our body to God (1 Cor. 6:20). Jesus' eyes were opened to the Bible to see that He was the growth of Abraham's tent:

Your father Abraham rejoiced to see my day: and he saw it, and was glad (John 8:56)

Also, Jesus' ears were opened to the Bible, to hear that He was the enlargement of the Father's temple:

Mine ears hast thou opened… Then said I, Lo, I come: in the volume of the book it is written of me (Ps. 40:6,7).

Therefore, He willingly gave His body to the Father, as it is written afterward:

Then said I, Lo, I come, (in the volume of the book it is written of me,) to do thy will, O God (Heb. 10:7)

The spirit of this passage from Psalm 40 and its quotation in Hebrews 10, actually permeates the Bible and we will examine how this is. Before, however, we must note something foundational.

There tends to be two main groups among Bible believers. The one group believes in the literal interpretation more than the spiritual interpretation. The other group tends to the opposite, believing that the Bible speaks more for spiritualizing purposes and less for literal interpretation. Uniquely, within each of these two groups themselves, all have differences from each other, as to what is literal, versus symbolic or spiritual.

However, God is often speaking on many levels at the same time in the Bible. In such cases the literal and the spiritual are not mutually exclusive but inlay each other. It is even found that there are layers of literal and layers of spiritual embodied in each other, giving tremendous dimensional attribute to one single passage. This occurs more often in the Bible than both groups prefer to realize.

In Psalm 40 we have this dimensional inlay. When the Psalmist says, *"in the volume of the book it is written of me (Ps. 40:7),"* he is speaking literally of himself. In context, the Psalmist views himself as one who the Bible writes about, as someone who delights to do God's will and keep God's law in his heart (vs. 8).

In Hebrews 10, there is a deeper layer. When the author of Hebrews quotes, *"in the volume of the book it is written of me (vs. 7),"* he is speaking beyond the Psalmist to the person of Christ, based on the context. As such, we see that the Psalm 40 passage reveals a spiritual interpretation abiding within the literal interpretation.

In such ways, the Spirit goes beyond the author's intentions and the passage context. The more layered the interpretations the Spirit has sown the more it eludes traditional interpretation measures to discern.

With this in mind, we find yet, even more literal and spiritual layers of fulfillment in Psalm 40:7, in the words, *"I come: in the volume of the book it is written of me."*

The words *"I come,"* infers an appearing in the future, speaking of Jesus.

By adding the words *"in the volume of the book"* infers that the future appearing of Jesus will be in the Bible.

By adding again, the words *"it is written of me,"* infers that the future appearing of Jesus in the Bible will be His testimony.

In summary, the Bible, which is the volume of the book, testifies to Jesus, the Word made flesh, appearing in a human body to fulfill God's will of the tabernacle and the offerings. Not only do the words speak so in a letter by letter way, but the entirety of the Bible forms a pictogram to the same testimony. This further layer of interpretation is dimensional and is prophetic: *for the testimony of Jesus is the spirit of prophecy (Rev. 19:10)*.

When it comes to these deep layers of interpretation, we cannot say that because the author was not intending a pictogram, or the context is not intending a pictogram, therefore the Spirit was not intending a pictogram. With all of this fresh in mind, we will go directly into the next chapter to examine the Bible as a pictogram of the human body and atonement of Jesus Christ. Through a series of fifteen different pictograms, we will see what only a finished Bible can reveal, *"...a body hast thou prepared me (Heb. 10:5)."*

CHAPTER 16

A BODY HAST THOU PREPARED ME 2

WHEREFORE WHEN HE COMETH INTO
THE WORLD, HE SAITH, SACRFICE AND
OFFERING THOU WOULDEST NOT, BUT A
BODY HAST THOU PREPARED ME

HEBREWS 10:5

Pictogram 1: From scroll to book, from DNA to body.

The seed of the Bible was in the form of scrolls, particularly the Old Testament, *"Take thee a roll of a book… (Jer. 36:2,4,32)."* The maturity of the Bible is now in book form. We are seeing all the more that the King James Bible is that matured book.

Outwardly, their shapes and content look very different from each other, yet both the source scrolls and the final book contain the same writings because they are of each other, albeit enhancements have now surfaced. Just like a scroll, the human DNA double helix has its content in spiral shape. This wound up DNA has all the coding necessary to eventually manifest a complex body. However, it needs a translator known as messenger RNA to complete the maturity process by reading and interpreting the code for gene expression. In this process is determined DNA word grouping and punctuation marks in the genetic code. This translation defines meaning, and, start and stop points for the accurate outworking of the source code into a functional product.

So in like manner, the scroll of the prophet Isaiah, for example, began spiraled with Hebrew coding but has now matured into a book in English by necessary means of translation. This book comes from the DNA of a scroll, and by maturing steps now makes up a part of the perfect expression of the finished Bible, *"the volume of the book (Heb. 10:7)."* Also, like DNA, the by and large of both the Hebrew and Greek scriptures had no spaces or punctuation marks. Without such start and stop markers, discernment issues are presented. Like messenger RNA, the interpreting Holy Spirit has performed all editing in the matter with English punctuating marks and word spacing. There will be no second estimating His translation of the King James Bible in content or shape.

This is a simplification of both the DNA process of the human body and the development of the body of the Bible but serves still to represent the relationship.

Pictogram 2: Right side left side paradigm.

When the scrolls' contents of Hebrew code matured into an English book through inspiration, unique developments manifested. One such development was a right side left side paradigm, just like the human body.

Picture, if you will, the famous drawing of "The Vitruvian Man" by Leonardo da Vinci, which depicts the blend of mathematics and art in the design of the human body. The Bible also has a very clearly defined right side and left side, with its demarcation of the New Testament and Old Testament.

The scrolls, as the premature DNA of the Bible could never manifest this bodily attribute of sides, but they did carry the mathematical component for it to come. This is because the nature of a scroll is to be wound up and unrolled and not to have a clearly defined center. A book, on the other hand, is opened split wide and plainly shows its right side left side feature. This final expression of God, dividing the Bible with its two sides, is very artistic, as is the human body.

Pictogram 3: Right side dominate trait.

The mathematical seed of the scrolls, which grew into the artistic revelation of the body of the book of the Bible, have strong right sided, dispositional, predetermination, like the human body.

The right side left side paradigm carries an absolute strength biased in its right side, which is the New Testament. For example, where is the law found? Of course, it is the left side, in the Old Testament. Can anyone be justified by the works of the law (Gal. 2:16)? The answer is no. Clearly, the overwhelming majority of mankind is not left handed. To attempt to live by their left hand would only cause stumbling (Rom. 9:32).

And where is the Spirit given? Of course, it is the right side, in the New Testament, where we have the hearing of faith. We can sum this side up as the "right hand" of the Bible. We have already seen in chapters past that the Bible is in God's right hand and Jesus is at God's right hand (Rev. 5:1,7). Throughout scripture, dozens of times, God is always referring to His right hand as His saving and providing hand:

Fear thou not; For I am with thee: be not dismayed; for I am thy God: I will strengthen thee; yea, I will uphold thee with the right hand of my righteousness (Isa. 41:10)

He will train His own to be right handed as well…

For I the Lord thy God will hold thy right hand, saying unto thee, Fear not; I will help thee (Isaiah 41:13)

Literally speaking, by this we know that Jesus is without question right handed. Spiritually speaking, by this we know that when Jesus fulfilled all righteousness, it was considered an act by His right hand.

At the same time, we would never say we do not need our left hand. Neither would we say we do not need the left side of the Bible. Even as our left hand is very useful in supporting the right hand in many tasks, so if we are to accurately interpret the New Testament, we need the minor supporting role of the Old Testament. If you are majoring in the Old Testament as your understanding of the word of God, and the New Testament is only the lending side, then you are left handed and you are stumbling whether you know it or not.

Pictogram 4: The spine.

There has never been a point in time when the original Hebrew Old Testament and the original Greek New Testament came together bound in a single volume. A final Bible, from beginning to end, carrying the inspiration of the originals has only happened in the English Bible. For this, a spine was required.

In the middle chapter of the King James Bible we have this spine, which is Psalm 117. There is an exact number of chapters to the right and an exact number of chapters to the left of this Psalm. Also, this happens to be the shortest chapter of the Bible with only two verses:

> *O praise the Lord, all ye nations: praise him, all ye people. For his merciful kindness is great toward us: and the truth of the Lord endureth for ever. Praise ye the Lord (Psalm 117)*

This spine chapter of the Bible has precisely thirty-three words which is one word for each vertebra as found in the spine of the human body. This is very meaningful.

The spine is the backbone of the human body. Without a backbone there is no standing. By representing the backbone with thirty-three vertebra matching words, God has declared that *"the truth of the Lord endureth for ever (vs. 2)."*

Meaningful again is that the spine is the backbone of the book. This means it is in touch with every page of the book and likewise every page is also connected in to the spine. The book of Genesis does not touch the book of Revelation, but they are still connected through the spine of the Bible. This is highly representative of how the human body has all its members in connection through the central nervous system which runs through the spinal column.

Just like I can take my right hand and reach over and touch my left hand, I can take the pages of Genesis and make them reach to touch the pages of Revelation, in both cases we mean this in an outward sense. But it is really through the spine that they have connection. The spine signifies that they belong together in an inward sense. This is why there is so much mysterious cross referencing in the Bible. This could never be the case for a scroll. As you opened it you were simultaneously closing it by rolling up the read portion. Therefore, the scrolls could not mimic the human body, only the genetics.

We are beginning to see the layers of prophetic and dimensional interpretations sowed by the Spirit in the Bible. The common theme we are examining is the finished Bible itself as yet another layer of fulfillment of the words about Jesus, *"a body hast thou prepared me (Heb. 10:5)."*

We have thus far seen that the Bible had a scrolled DNA which manifested maturity in the body of a book. This matured body has a right side and a left side just like our body. Like mankind, the strength and skill are in the right hand. There is also a spine that reaches to all the members of its body and connects them all to each other. We will continue this examination immediately in the next chapter.

CHAPTER 17

A Body Hast Thou Prepared Me 3

BEHOLD, THOU DESIREST TRUTH
IN THE INWARD PARTS: AND
IN THE HIDDEN PART THOU SHALT
MAKE ME TO KNOW WISDOM

PSALM 51:6

Pictogram 5: Chromosomes.

As we began the topic "A Body Hast Thou Prepared Me" two chapters ago, we spoke of the human body as the enlargement of the true temple of God. Solomon's temple was grand standing, but the body of Jesus was greater yet for the in dwelling place of the Father.

Before modern science told us that the human body has 46 chromosomes, God already did. In the porch of Solomon's temple were two great pillars of brass, named Jachin and Boaz (1 Kings 7:21). These standing pillars were measured out by God:

> *For he cast two pillars of brass, of eighteen cubits high apiece... And he made two chapiters of molten brass, to set upon the tops of the pillars: the height*

of the one chapiter was five cubits, and the height of the other chapiter was five cubits (1 Kings 7:15,16)

Each pillar, with its cap, was a total of twenty-three cubits. They stood side by side equaling together, forty-six cubits. This has the same appearance of the DNA ladders and is an exact representation of the forty-six chromosomes of the human being. In the case of DNA, like the pillar cubits, there are twenty-three chromosomes on one side contributed by the mother, and twenty-three chromosomes on the other side contributed by the father. In the last chapter we talked about the scrolled nature of the DNA double helix which makes up the chromosomes. We want to ad quickly that in Solomon's temple was a spiraled stair case leading to upper levels of the temple, *"…and they went up with winding stairs into the middle chamber, and out of the middle into the third (1 Kings 6:8)."* This was a great testimony in front and inside of Solomon's sanctuary telling that God would be coming in a human body.

When God did come in Christ, He was already done with Solomon's temple. That which represented the human chromosomes was now replaced with actual human chromosomes. Based on this, He was mix communicating and speaking over their heads when He engaged the Jews:

Jesus answered and said unto them, Destroy this temple, and in three days I will raise it up. Then said the Jews, Forty and six years was this temple in building, and wilt thou rear it up in three days? But he spake of the temple of his body (John 2:19-21)

The temple took forty-six years to build. This is a second testimony to the issue of the Bible containing the pictogram of the chromosomes of the human body.

It is very important to see that the human body is the temple of God if you are born again. Two times we are told this in simple black and white letters by the Apostle Paul in the book of 1 Corinthians:

Know ye not that ye are the temple of God, and that the Spirit of God dwelleth in you? (1 Cor. 3:16)

And again…

What? Know ye not that your body is the temple of the Holy Ghost which is in you, which ye have of God, and ye are not your own? (1 Cor. 6:19)

Why did God wait until the book of 1 Corinthians to speak so plainly? These two verses together make a third testimony to the chromosomal representation in the finished Bible, as the book of 1 Corinthians is the forty-sixth book in the chronological order of the canon of the Bible. This too was intentional by God.

Along this line of revelation, there is only one detailed account in the Bible of the birth of Jesus, the Word made flesh. It is well accounted in Luke chapter two, which is the forty-sixth chapter of the New Testament:

And she brought forth her firstborn son, and wrapped him in swaddling clothes, and laid him in a manger; because there was no room for them in the inn (Chapter 46 of the NT, Luke 2:7)

And…

For unto you is born this day in the city of David a Saviour, which is Christ the Lord (Chapter 46 of the NT, Luke 2:11)

Not only does the Spirit give us this double testimony, but in the forty-sixth verse of the forty-sixth chapter of the New Testament, we read this:

And it came to pass, that after three days they found him in the temple, sitting in the midst of the doctors, both hearing them and asking them questions (Chapter 46 of the NT, Luke 2:46)

The Spirit gives us an incredible double entendre: Literally speaking, this verse tells us that Jesus was found in the temple of Solomon. However, also literally speaking on a deeper layer, Jesus was found in the temple of the body. This latter appraisal gives a loaded meaning to, *"they found him in the temple (Verse 46)."* Most interestingly, the Spirit uses the word *"doctors."* This is absolutely referring to Doctor of the law. However again, spiritually speaking, the Spirit chose a word that lends to the impression of medical doctors examining God in a body. This is a prime example of the oft occurring prophetic and dimensional interpretation that we prefer not to realize.

Going back in order, God loaded the Bible with chromosomes from the beginning. Because Eve was genetically taken out of man, in Genesis 2:23,24 Adam was allotted forty-six words to describe his chromosomal match:

> *This is now bone of my bones, and flesh of my flesh: she shall be called woman, because she was taken out of man. Therefore shall a man leave his father and his mother, and shall cleave unto his wife: and they shall be one flesh*

You will only find this in the King James Bible because it alone is the matured, finished Bible carrying the inspiration of God.

You should also know that Satan goes straight to the chromosomes to alter life. When he took down Adam and Eve in Genesis 3:1,4,5 he stung their chromosomes with the infusion of sin. Therefore, he too was allotted only forty-six words as well:

> *Yea, hath God said, Ye shall not eat of every tree of the garden?*

> *Ye shall not surely die: For God doth know that in the day ye eat thereof, then your eyes shall be opened, and ye shall be as gods, knowing good and evil*

You should also know that Satan is going after the chromosomes of the word of God, the King James Bible, to alter life again.

Certainly, this issue is wrapped up in the number forty-six. Only the finished Bible could manifest such detail. If your Bible does not have these details, it is a genetically modified organism.

You may appreciate the Bible for its outward revelation, praise God! But God is not satisfied with a surface level Bible. He desires the truth of His testimony to run deep in the inward parts of the Bible. He wants not only an outer perfection of doctrine but truth in the hidden part of the Bible as well. He is making this wisdom known to you in this book.

CHAPTER 18

A BODY HAST THOU PREPARED ME 4

FOR HE IS OUR PEACE, WHO HATH MADE BOTH ONE, AND HATH BROKEN DOWN THE MIDDLE WALL OF PARTITION BETWEEN US... AND THAT HE MIGHT RECONCILE BOTH UNTO GOD IN ONE BODY BY THE CROSS, HAVING SLAIN THE ENMITY THEREBY

EPHESIANS 2:14, 16

Pictogram 6: The gospels, the rungs of DNA.

Even a first-time reader of the Bible will soon enough identify that the two sides, the Old Testament and the New Testament, come across very different from each other. They stand like two people who should belong together yet have a disagreement between them. This disagreement is their antithetical natures of law and faith, letter and Spirit, works and grace, and the likes.

Furthermore, the four gospels are also very different from the Old and New Testament, which they come between in the chronology of the Bible.

Matthew, Mark, Luke and John stand uniquely alone, all covering the same thing, the life of Christ. Herein is the reconciliation of the Old and New Testament.

When we mix and match parts of Matthew, Mark, Luke and John, we gain all sorts of details and features regarding the life of Christ. We also gain a better insight into the Old Testament on the one side and the New Testament on the other. The gospels actually make a bridge for these two opposites and join what is harshly different by providing a middle blend. Christ in the gospels is the peace maker who upholds the truth of the two parties He stands between.

In human physiology we have the same thing at work. When the twenty-three chromosomes of one parent are introduced with the twenty-three chromosomes of the opposite parent, they await a joining agent who will make peace of both sides. Apart from this they will remain alone because they are otherwise very different from each other.

This joining of a maternal side with a paternal side is specifically what takes place on the DNA level. Remembering from the last chapter the spiraled stair case in Solomon's temple, we picture the spiraled double helix of DNA. As the stair case has steps, so the DNA has rungs that are joining each opposite side of its ladder. These rungs are always made up of the same four nucleic acids: Adenine, Thymine, Cytosine and Guanine. These are the four gospels of human DNA which join each parental side together into a seamless blend.

Even as Matthew, Mark, Luke and John combine with each other to reveal so many great insights through their synergy, so Adenine, Thymine, Cytosine and Guanine are always joining each other to make the base pair rungs which join the two DNA strands. These base pair steps are the letters that spell out the many details of the human being to come. This DNA winding stair case will turn one revolution per ten rungs, or steps, to form the visual we have in mind when we picture DNA. By no coincidence, beginning with the verse that reveals the winding stair case of Solomon's temple as noted in the last chapter, the King James Bible uses the word "stairs" a grand total of ten times to match the DNA twist (1 Ki. 6:8; 2 Ki. 9:13; Ne. 3:15; 9:4; 12:37; SS 2:14; Eze. 40:6; 43:17; Ac 21:35; 21:40).

Pictogram 7: The gospels, the heart of the body.

When someone begins to seek after Christ, it is most common the experience to open the Bible to Matthew, Mark, Luke and John. This is because it is the heart of the Bible.

In the body, the heart is considered the central muscle. When a person is suspected to have died, the first thing someone will do is check for a heartbeat, then a pulse. Checking for a pulse is a secondary verification of the heart's status.

The heart is made up of four chambers: right and left atriums; right and left ventricles. The right atrium receives the cycled blood of the body from the veins and pumps it to the right ventricle. This ventricle pumps it to the lungs to be imbibed with fresh oxygen. The left atrium receives it back from the lungs and pumps it to the left ventricle. The left ventricle then pumps this high-quality blood back to the body.

Likewise, in the heart of the Bible we have the pumping of oxygen enriched blood. The crucifixion of Jesus, recorded in the four gospels, gives the entire body of the Bible its heartbeat. If you rip the gospels out of the Bible, you tear out its heart and it becomes dead and lifeless, and we too are then dead in our sins. But how is the blood of Calvary oxygenated? It is made so through the supply of the Spirit: *"...the blood of Christ, who through the eternal Spirit offered himself without spot to God... Heb. 9:14."*

Did you catch that? This verse associates *"the blood of Christ"* and *"the eternal Spirit."* In the Bible the Spirit represents air supply. The blood of the body of Christ was received and pumped through with the breath of the Spirit and then pumped to the Father. This is how, *"by his own blood (vs. 12),"* Christ entered into the Father to propitiate for our sins. This blood was received, and then pumped back to the body of Christ, the church, in the New Testament for the supply of the Spirit of life.

Next, among the four chambers of the heart, one is stronger than the rest. This would be the left ventricle, which is the ultimate pumping chamber of oxygenated blood to the body. This correlates to the issue of the synoptic gospels. In short, this issue is the content match of Matthew, Mark and Luke's recording of the life of Christ. John makes a departure, and though he still captures the life of Christ, it is profoundly more powerful in its coverage. This gospel stands out from the other three as the strongest since it singly emphasizes the deity of Christ.

Pictogram 8: The blood, the life of the body.

Closely related to the issue of the heart of the Bible is the blood that it is pumping through its circulatory system from Genesis to Revelation.

The Bible is saturated with the topic of "the blood" because the Bible is saturated with the topic of the forgiveness of sins.

For the life of the flesh is in the blood: and I have given it to you upon the altar to make an atonement for your souls: for it is the blood that maketh an atonement for the soul (Lev. 17:11)

We previously saw in the last pictogram that the blood of Christ was oxygenated by the eternal Spirit to then make atonement to the Father. By the eternal Spirit's oxygenating the blood of Christ in order to present to the Father, it means that the Holy Spirit was in agreement with the perfection of the life and death sacrifice of Christ to atone for souls, *"Great is the mystery of Godliness: God was manifest in the flesh, justified in the Spirit (1 Tim. 3:16)."*

From there, this Godhead sanctified blood was pumped back out from the heart muscle of the Bible (Matthew, Mark, Luke, John). Even as the body's heart depends on the one strong chamber to do this massive work, so does the heart of the Bible. Post resurrection, we see the blood mixed with the oxygen (breath) of the Spirit being pumped back into the body of Christ by the stronger chamber of the gospel of John:

And when he had said this, he breathed on them, and saith unto them, Receive ye the Holy Ghost: Whose soever sins ye remit, they are remitted unto them; and whose soever sins ye retain, they are retained (John 20:22,23)

In these verses we have the *"Holy Ghost"* followed by *"Whose soever sins ye remit"*. In between is a colon, which means there is a direct relationship. The Holy Ghost is the Spirit, or air, or breath, meaning oxygen. The remittance of sins is the blood.

Truly this blood is most unique and corresponds to the human bodies blood type O Negative. Let's look into this next.

Like the heart and its four chambers, the blood also has a four-type designation. This would be the body's four main blood types which are A, B, AB and O.

While not just any blood type can donate to save a body, there is one that is uniquely able to do so. The O Negative blood type is different from all the rest in this way and is called a universal donor. This means that any blood type can receive this blood in emergency. In other words, this blood is for the saving of all mankind.

This universal blood type is unique because it is the blood of God. Just as the four chambers of the heart had one stronger than the rest and the four blood types have one unique from the rest, so the gospels have one that is set apart from the other three. Again, it is the gospel of John because of its emphasis on the deity of Christ. God is providing blood that is qualified as the universal donor type for the remission of sins:

Take heed therefore unto yourselves, and to all the flock, over the which the Holy Ghost hath made you overseers, to feed the church of God, which he hath purchased with his own blood (Acts 20:28)

All mankind is dependent on this blood transfusion. If you do not believe in the deity of Jesus Christ you have another gospel, you do not have the blood type you need. You are accursed and will die in your sins, much like one who receives the wrong type of blood (Gal. 1:9). The first sign of receiving the wrong blood type in a transfusion is a feeling of impending doom. This is a legitimate medical symptom and aptly fits the one who rejects the deity of Jesus Christ into their life.

In a whole other sense, the Bible is not O Negative blood type, but AB Positive. This blood type is called the universal receiver. This means that it can take into itself any blood type without experiencing ill affect. In other words, there are no colors, races or ethnicities amongst the sons of men who Christ would reject from being washed in His blood, *"All that the Father giveth me shall come to me; and him that cometh to me I will in no wise cast out (John 6:37)."* He can receive and take into His blood all types without concern of polluting His own blood stream in the process. Therefore, the church is made up of all nationalities:

> *After this, I beheld, and, lo, a great multitude, which no man could number, of all nations, and kindreds, and people, and tongues, stood before the throne, and before the Lamb, clothed with white robes, and palms in their hands (Rev. 7:9)*

We have now seen many more of the Bibles pictograms of the body of Jesus. We saw before, that the Bible had a scrolled DNA which manifested maturity in the body of a book. This body has a right side and a left side, but its strength is in the right hand. This body of a book has a thirty-three-word middle chapter just like the vertebra of the spine. Now we have added its core attribute of forty-six chromosomes. This is the core level where we, in our body, are affected by sin from generation to generation. However, the true body of the Bible, the King James Bible, is not affected on this level, or any level. The very rungs of the Bible's DNA are manifesting a perfect genetic work in the Old and New Testament joined by the gospels. The heart beat is strong, and the blood is divine.

This is the pictogram of the Bible as the human body of Jesus and it continues in the next chapter.

CHAPTER 19

A Body Hast Thou Prepared Me 5

For Dogs Have Compassed Me: The Assembly Of The Wicked Have Inclosed Me: They Pierced My Hands And My Feet

Psalm 22:16

Pictogram 9: The Bible and the immune system

The immune system is the body's defender against bacteria, microbes, viruses, toxins, parasites, etc. which amount to infectious disease. The power of the immune system is much more than realized by us from day to day. If you were to die, your immune system would shut down instantly, and you would be invaded by a massive swarm of organisms. These organisms would dismantle you and reduce you to a skeleton in just a matter of weeks.

While a body is living it is amazing how this dismantling is kept from happening. If the Bible did not have an immune system, it could not have gone from seed, through growth and into maturity in the King James

Bible. Furthermore, the KJV could not have lasted four hundred years without adverse changes.

When the 1611 King James Bible came forth, on the one hand it was a maturity. On the other hand, it was like a birth. The internal immune system that had been working it through history would now continue to operate in this living organism more than ever.

As a newborn of a kind, by virtue of its long standing immune system guarding inspiration from the beginning, it had reached a homeostasis. This is the term used to describe the health stability of anything living in relation to its internal components.

This is not to say that the Bible has ever had an ailment of its own nature. However, the word of God entering this world required an agent to fight off the demise of this world, which would attempt to enter its system by both man and Devil. I cannot emphasize this point enough and advise you to reread this, till it sinks in thoroughly.

Here are some very simple examples of the Bible's immune system at work:

Freemasonry: The history long Satanic cult of Freemasonry made great attempt to adorn the 1611 King James Bible with secret society art work. You may not be familiar with this fact because quickly on, the KJV immune system purged this from its pages. We could compare this mockery to what Jesus went through when He was covered in a purple robe and had a crown of thorns placed upon His head.

The Apocrypha: In between the Old and New Testament of the 1611 King James Bible were a host of books titled, "The Apocrypha." The King James translators included these books as historical writings. They never meant them to be considered inspired scripture, hence the name "The Apocrypha," which means, "not the writings." In time, the Bible's immune system rejected these books from its inclusion, though you can still buy copies of the KJV which have intentionally kept this in. The book of Isaiah is the immune system's response to the Apocrypha. It contains sixty-six chapters which form a micro Bible, the Bible itself containing sixty-six books. The contents of each chapter of Isaiah match the contents of each book of the Bible in chronological order. This leaves no room for the Apocrypha. The Bible has fought off the Apocrypha via its immune system. We will be examining the topic of Isaiah's matching chapters to the Bible's books in great detail toward the end of this book.

Typos: When the 1611 KJV was printed, this was a real feat for its time. The advent of printing was in its infancy, as was the King James Bible. Each word was hand type set, letter by letter, and backwards. Such was the technology of the day. To complicate matters, the printing process was slow and required various printing houses. So as example, the gospel of John could have had a typo in one passage and not in another. The same gospel of John from another printing house could have not made an error in the same place but have done so in a completely different area. From one printing house to the next, over the years, all human induced spelling errors needed to be expunged. This was the job of the Bible's immune system to eradicate any contribution that was not the pure inbreeding of the Holy Spirit.

Spelling: Also, in time, the spelling of many words changed in the formal printing of the King James Bible. It is important to understand that the words did not change but only the spelling of the same words. This was in harmony with the shaping of the English language all in all. This is a maturity feature.

Font: The font was originally a very fancy Gothic font. For ease of reading, this has also changed to more of a Roman text, typically speaking. This is not necessarily an issue requiring the immune system but still worth mentioning. Again, no words have been changed. If you would fluently read the 1611 KJV and a KJV purchased today, the simultaneous reading would be in tandem.

These are just some examples of the King James Bible's immune system at work. Before you condemn the word of God, reconsider instead how the immune system is at work to protect the body.

Pictogram 10: Bound in leather, the skin of the body

It might seem unbelievable that God would even put cosmetic detail to the finished Bible, such as a leather cover. However, we must remember that all of these pictograms are because of one truth, *"the word was made flesh (John 1:14)."* Christ came wrapped in skin and so did the finished Bible.

Bibles come in leather covers in many different colors. There are Bibles in white skin, black skin, red skin, brown skin, tan skin, etc., etc. This is symbolic of the body of Christ made up from all skin colors, filled with the word of Christ, *"Let the word of Christ dwell in you richly in all wisdom (Col. 3;16)."* In case you think this is an exaggeration, you need to know that this was even prophesied through the life of Joseph:

Now Israel loved Joseph more than all his children, because he was the son of his old age: and he made him a coat of many colours (Gen. 37:3)

Joseph is a prophetic type of Christ in the Bible. Even as Joseph's father covered him in *"a coat of many colours,"* so the Father has covered the body of Christ with many skin colors. In as much as this word in Gen. 37:3 is true of Jesus, the Word of God, so it is true of the Bible, the word of God.

Here again we encounter the depth and layer of dimensional interpretation that is very inconvenient to our pre-conceived theological grid.

With this pictogram of skin for skin, we are shifting to more of the outward appearances of the Bible as the human body.

Pictogram 11: The Bible has hands

If you put your hands, palms up, before your face, you will read from left to right the following: One thumb, then four fingers, four fingers again, then one thumb again.

If we convert that into straight numbers, we have "1 4 4 1." When God finished the Bible, He signified its hands by making every single scripture that contains "1 4 4 1" in its address, to deal with the work of the hands.

Psalm 144:1 says, *"Blessed be the Lord my strength, which teacheth my hands to war, and my fingers to fight."*

Mark 14:41 says, *"And he cometh the third time, and saith unto them, Sleep on now, and take your rest: it is enough, the hour is come; behold, the Son of man is betrayed into the hands of sinners."*

Numbers 14:41 deals with transgressing the commandment of the Lord, which ultimately traces back to the hand-written commandments by the finger of God. Leviticus 14:41 deals with the sanitary scraping of the house which has the plague of leprosy. 1 Samuel 14:41 deals with the casting of lots. All of these involve the hands.

These are the five verses in the entire Bible that have "1 4 4 1" in the addresses and they all have to do with the acts of the hand. This set of five verses would be the demarcation of the 5 fingers on the human hand, 4 Old Testament and 1 New Testament, that's 4 fingers and 1 thumb.

Pictogram 12: The Bible has feet

A good verse to take us from the subject of hands to feet is Daniel 10:10 where we read about "10" fingers and "10" toes touching the ground. This numeric display directly matches the verse address:

And, behold, an hand touched me, which set me upon my knees and upon the palms of my hands (Dan. 10:10)

This is another example of how the finished Bible has multiplied order upon order and detail upon detail. This passage though, is not what we are referring to when we say that the Bible has feet.

The finished Bible's feet can only be found in the King James Bible. They are seen in the first and last verse of the Bible. These are the two verses that the Bible stands upon like the feet of the body.

The left foot:

In the beginning God created the heaven and the earth (Gen. 1:1)

The right foot:

The grace of our Lord Jesus Christ be with you all. Amen (Rev. 22:21)

This first and last verse of the King James Bible each have 44 letters. This first and last verse of the King James Bible each have 27 consonants also. And this first and last verse of the King James Bible each have 17 vowels also. These feet have balance to stand. And these feet are the feet of Jesus who tells us Himself, *"I am Alpha and Omega, the beginning and the ending (Rev. 1:8)."* Furthermore, to prove these feet of 44 letters in the first verse and 44 letters in the last verse are God's feet, which are the *"beginning (Rev. 1:8)"* and *"ending (Rev. 1:8)"* of the KJV, the word "God" is written exactly 4444 times in the King James Bible, which is a 44 (left foot) and a 44 (right foot) standing together. In fact, the word "God" is not only written 4444 times, it is the actual 4444'th word, and the actual 444'th word and the actual 4'th word in the King James Bible.

We saw four particular revelations in this chapter which were the immune system, the skin, and the hands and feet. The immune system of the Bible is a tremendous defender against the defilement of the world, the flesh and the Devil. However, the immune system is not designed to ward away being nailed to a cross. When this took place, the skin of Jesus was torn for mankind to enter into God's presence through *"the veil"* of *"His flesh (Heb. 10:20)."* Each time we crack open the Bible we reenact the crucifixion of Jesus by parting its skin cover in order to enter God's presence. Also, to this, knowing from a previous ago chapter that the Bible in seed form was nailed to the cross above Jesus' head, and knowing what we know now from this chapter, we have a whole other level to the prophecy, *"They pierced my hands and my feet (Psalm 22:16)."*

CHAPTER 20

A Body Hast Thou Prepared Me 6

He Hath Made Every Thing Beautiful In His Time: Also He Hath Set The World In Their Heart, So That No Man Can Find Out The Work That God Maketh From The Beginning To The End

Ecclesiastes 3:11

By this point in the journey of "A Body Hast Thou Prepared Me," we should give recognition to the phenomena that a facsimile of the human body is emerging from the finished Bible. To reiterate, this is a witness of the Spirit that *"the word was made flesh (John 1:14)."*

We have seen excerpts from the author of Hebrews; the prophets Jeremiah and Isaiah; the apostles Paul and John; the man of God Moses; Luke, Adam, Nehemiah; the prophet Ezekiel; Joseph and Mark; the man of God Samuel; and the prophet Daniel.

What seems like totally random contributions by men is actually more like complicated gene editing by the Spirit, to bring forth a God glorifying mosaic of the human body and divine ministry of Jesus Christ, through the King James Bible. Even Satan was forced to contribute and give glory to God in this way. This entire process reminds us of the truth of His eternal power and Godhead:

And we know that all things work together for good to them that love God, to them who are the called according to his purpose (Rom. 8:28)

I am most impressed with the Spirit's work in the last three pictograms ahead, as they are the epitome of the testimony of Jesus.

Pictogram 13: Sentences are stripes

So often, we are not satisfied with God's answers. We start our Christian pilgrimage with the faith of a child and then we become very complicated in the middle years. If we persevere, we reach the Father and we end where we started, with the faith of the child, but in a matured form. The Apostle John covers this:

I write unto you, little children, because your sins are forgiven you for his name's sake. I write unto you, fathers, because ye have known him that is from the beginning. I write unto you, young men, because ye have overcome the wicked one (1 John 2:12,13)

The children are children, they know God instinctually and are ready to be taught. The fathers are fathers and have a very deep knowing and oneness with God. They are simple and profound, and a little bit of God goes a long way in them. But the young men are young men and they are the teenagers of the house of God, and the ones who are the hardest to get through to. You can show them, but they do not see because they have a very strong mind of their own. They have *"overcome the wicked one,"* which means they have a very strong "fight" mentality (Ephesians 6:10-18).

Children in the household of God will read this book and immediately recognize with a simple and pure mind, that the King James Bible is the seed of God. It will make obvious sense to them because children connect with the basics and can see the wonder in it all without prejudice. The truth will easily nest in their hearts. Fathers in the household of God will sense a deep spiritual current towing them into wisdom when reading this book. They will be ready to see that the Father is rewarding them, and they can laugh at themselves for being deceived for so long by counterfeit Bibles. They will sigh and confess with God and receive knowledge, *"yea, let God be true, but every man a liar; as it is written (Rom. 3:4)."*

If you have been wrestling with this book, please continue to do so. You are still a young man. This stage cannot be bypassed in becoming a father. Fathers are not ardent but soft toward God when He corrects them, even insulting their intellect. Do not think you are too experienced a pastor, therefore you are a Father. Do not think you have been a faithful Christian for decades, therefore you are a father. Neither the appointing of men, nor the passing of time can deliver you into maturity. Only the endowment of the Spirit deeply wrought through your spirit can bring forth a Father.

Therefore, young men will not likely see any truth in the simplicity in these last pictograms. However, the truth of the matter is that the most profound things of God are right in front of our eyes the whole time, like the finished Bible.

Such is the case with the actual sentences that are written in the Bible. Line after line they are striping the page. These stripes are the stripes of Christ:

But he was wounded for our transgressions, he was bruised for our iniquities: the chastisement of our peace was upon him; and with his stripes we are healed (Isaiah 53:5)

The Bible is bearing about in its body the stripes of Christ that He bore on His back. The striped back of Jesus was first shown to Moses. Remember that the human back has thirty-three vertebrae, therefore it is was shown to him in chapter thirty-three of Exodus:

And it shall come to pass, while my glory passeth by, that I will put thee in a clift of the rock, and will cover thee with my hand while I pass by: And I will take away mine hand, and thou shalt see my back parts: but my face shall not be seen (Exodus 33:22,23)

Moses saw the back side of Christ, the glory of God, the stripes of Jesus. On the day of the crucifixion, the people of Jerusalem also saw the stripes of Jesus, the glory of God, the back of Christ. Today, each time someone opens the Bible, whether they have eyes to see or not, there is the same revelation of God before them.

This correlation is so subtle. If you doubt what you are seeing, you will miss it. In a split second, unbelief will rob you of this revelation forever.

Pictogram 14: Pages are trees

Continuing in the spirit of the most profound things of God being the easiest to overlook, and the hardest to appreciate, we learn of God:

My doctrine shall drop as the rain, my speech shall distil as the dew, as the small rain upon the tender herb, and as the showers upon the grass (Deut. 32:2)

The *"dew"* and *"the small rain"* will *"distil"* themselves. This means they have the nature of appearing by an osmosis, and then they evaporate away. Their coming and going is mysterious and ghost like. In between their coming and going is a very fragile abiding presence that is gliding the *"tender herb"*, which signifies the heart (Isa. 53:2). If our heart is shaken with unbelief, the little drops will immediately roll off the blade and be gone. Such is the *"speech"* of God, and so is our hearing of the most powerful things He has to say. It is a true test of our maturity to be able to hear from God in this way.

Adding to the stripes of Christ on every page of the body of the Bible we have further details of His ministry of redemption:

Who his own self bare our sins in his own body on the tree, that we, being dead to sins, should live unto righteousness, by whose stripes ye were healed (1 Peter 2:24)

And...

Christ hath redeemed us from the curse of the law, being made a curse for us: for it is written, cursed is every one that hangeth on a tree (Gal. 3:13)

God's word began ink on skins but ended ink on paper. What is paper? Paper is tree.

To make paper from trees, we must first turn it into pulp. Incidentally, this is what happened to Jesus. His body was turned to pulp from judge and jury and executioner all the way to the cross. Through due process the pulp becomes paper and words are printed on it.

These printed words seem to be floating on the paper, or we could say hanging on the paper, or we could say, hanging on a tree. In the Bible, the word of God is hanging on a tree, just like Jesus the Word of God was hanging on a tree.

Don't let this vision blow away from you in the wind of the Spirit that has also brought it.

Pictogram 15: Red letter edition

Rubricating was a step in medieval manuscript making, whereby emphasized text was printed in red. It is almost a given that if you open any King James Bible today, you will find the words of Christ printed in red.

Despite detractors who would say otherwise, the 1611 King James Bible indeed had rubricating. However, it will not be found in the words of Christ but in the entry section.

This rubricating was a seed that the Spirit planted in the opening notes of the 1611 KJV. Then, alas, in the early 1900's, the words of Christ were printed in red. This was the maturing of the Spirit's 1611 seed and red-letter Bibles went mainstream.

This furthering of the Bible was the furthering of the expression of Christ's sacrifice on the cross. It is common Bible knowledge that "eight" is the number associated with Jesus and there are now a mere eight books in the New Testament alone sprinkled with red letters. With this sprinkling of red letters, the sprinkling of the blood of the sacrifice of Christ would forthwith come from the side of the Bible:

But one of the soldiers with a spear pierced his side, and forthwith came there out blood and water (John 19:34)

The blood was for redemption and the water was for the generating of the church:

Not by works of righteousness which we have done, but according to his mercy he saved us, by the washing of regeneration, and renewing of the Holy Ghost (Titus 3:5)

The word "church" is used exactly "eight-y" times in the King James Bible because it is the fruit of these eight books, which denote the blood and Spirit of Christ for the building of His body in the red letters. Eighty is the built-up number of eight even as the church is the built-up Christ (Eph. 1:23).

It was only a mere hundred years ago that this bloody detail manifested according to the seed in the notes of the 1611 King James Bible. This act of God in such close proximity to our generation should cause us to tremble at His presence in the matter regarding the doctrine of the Bible and how we hold it by faith. God is watching our every move and our every response regarding His King James Bible. If we see it left in antiquity, we have the doctrine of men and are not hearing from God. If we think God is not controlling His Bible, we have failed the test and have not the fear of the Lord. If we insist it is just a matter of translation, we have a low view of scripture and deceive ourselves. Feel God's impending closeness today, feel how real the King James Bible is as the actual word of God today, see Jesus Christ as Lord and Savior today, feel Heaven and Hell today. Fear God and the word of God, the 1611 KJV today.

Though many, many more pictograms depicting the King James Bible as the body and ministry of Christ exist, we will end with these fifteen. Men have been cast by God to be earth minded deep in their hearts, yet men are still accountable to Him for heavenly matters. No man can find out the works that God does from beginning to end, yet man will be responsible for knowing. No writer of the Bible understood what God was doing in the compilation and maturing of the King James Bible. Readers today scarcely understand either. God has made His word beautiful in His time, and He reveals it to whom He wills. Has He revealed it to you?

CHAPTER 21

EQUALITY OR TRUTH?

CALL UNTO ME, AND I WILL ANSWER THEE, AND SHEW THEE GREAT AND MIGHTY THINGS, WHICH THOU KNOWEST NOT

JEREMIAH 33:3

Having now read all about the anatomy of the Bible, we see just how fascinated God is with the human body. In the end, He considers it good enough for His own personal dwelling place. This is why He is taking it all the way into glorification (Rom. 8:30).

The KJV is also good enough for His dwelling place. This is why it is foolishness for a man to critique it. Up to now, we have seen many areas where all name brand Bibles manifest incredible patterns and configurations. Then we have seen beyond them into many further anomalies where only the King James version has arrangement. The King James Version will continue all the more to surge past the counterfeit name brand versions as this book continues. As this all comes to light, do not dismiss as phenomena, that which is the intelligent design of the creator.

Most likely, no matter who reads this book, things are being heard for the first time and like never before. The entire topic of the exclusivity of the

King James Bible as God's only inspired word today, likely, begs in you many deep questions about fairness of opportunity.

We must set the record straight: There is no such thing as equality with God. There is only the truth:

And the Lord said unto him, who hath made man's mouth? Or who maketh the dumb, or deaf, or the seeing, or the blind? Have not I the Lord? (Ex. 4:11)

And...

The Lord hath made all things for himself: yea, even the wicked for the day of evil (Prov. 16:4)

The above examples are all things we would not want to credit God for: the deaf, the dumb and the blind, and even the wicked. However, all are created by God intentionally the way they are, for the outworking of the truth of Himself, by grand demonstration: *"And as Jesus passed by, he saw a man which was blind from his birth... Jesus answered, Neither has this man sinned, nor his parents: but that the works of God should be made manifest in him (John 9:1-3)."*

To seek God through the lens of fairness rather than truth, is to never come to know Him. When the question arises in the heart, "is this fair?" we are thinking in a sinful man centered way, leaning on our own understanding (Prov. 3:5). We must rather ask, "is this true?" This is a holy God centered approach. Here are two very relatable to subject examples:

First, the Old Testament was written in Hebrew. If you did not know Hebrew, you needed a translator. If you did not have an interpreter, you could not know God. Eventually, translations of the Hebrew scriptures came into reach, such as the Septuagint, but they would always be a second-generation manuscript only as accurate as their translation, and never carrying inspiration. Therefore, if you were of the nations, you were handicapped from the start. Don't ask if this was fair. Rather, was this true?

> *And when the queen of Sheba heard of the fame of Solomon, she came to prove Solomon with hard questions at Jerusalem, with a very great company, and camels that bare spices, and gold in abundance, and precious stones: and when she was come to Solomon, she communed with him of all that was in her heart. And Solomon told her all her questions: and there was nothing hid from Solomon, which he told her not (2 Chron. 9:2)*

The queen of Sheba risked her life to travel from the far south up to Jerusalem to hear the truth of God she could only get from Israel. She did not say, "it is not fair," she was seeking to know, "is it true?"

> *And she said to the king, it was a true report which I heard in mine own land of thine acts, and of thy wisdom: Howbeit I believed not their words, until I came, and mine eyes had seen it: and behold, the one half of the greatness of thy wisdom was not told me: for thou exceedest the fame that I heard (vs. 5,6)*

Solomon is one of the greatest types of Jesus Christ in the Bible. Of example, he was the king of the Jews whose name means "Man of Peace," he had over a thousand wives and concubines, and he was the only one of the kings to never go to war. Jesus is the King of the Jews who is the "Prince of Peace," he has an innumerable bride in the church, and he will reign King of Kings in the thousand-year millennium of peace at the end of the age. This Christ is who the queen of Sheba was meeting.

And not only was she meeting the person of Christ displayed in Solomon, but she was meeting the word of God too. Remember, that Solomon wrote three of the sixty-six books of the Bible (Proverbs, Ecclesiastes, The Song of Solomon). Therefore, she was hearing the word of God which could only be found in Hebrew. Her response to her search upon discovering the truth of Jesus in Solomon and the very word of God in Solomon was pure, "*Blessed be the Lord thy God (vs. 8).*" Those were her words and her reaction.

Second, the New Testament was written in Greek. If you did not speak Greek, you were in the same scenario as described above. Again, it should not be asked regarding fairness to the rest of the world, as there is no such thing in God's economy, where all men are in the default position of deserving Hell. The only question is, "is it true?"

God is not doing anything different in our day than in days past. He relegated the truth to a seed in Hebrew in the day of the queen of Sheba. He grew this relegated seed in Greek in the early days of the church. He has now matured this relegated seed into English in the latter days of the church.

Christ, the head, has always spoken through a single major tongue and has given the same instructions to His body regarding the gift of tongues in the church:

If any man speak in an unknown tongue, let it be by two, or at the most by three, and that by course, and let one interpret (1 Cor. 14:27)

The uniformity of God in the matter of the Bible is identical. Written *"by course"* in Hebrew, Greek and a little Aramaic, *"two, or at the most by three."* Final authority then given in English, *"and let one interpret."*

To judge the matter of what is true regarding the Bible based on your own concept of equity, efficiency and fairness, is to not know God well, and to also miss God's actual moving. All of this at your own expense. Jesus said this speaking of the queen of Sheba:

The queen of the south shall rise up in the judgment with this generation, and shall condemn it: for she came from the uttermost parts of the earth to hear the wisdom of Solomon; and, behold, a greater than Solomon is here (Matt. 12:42)

Today, the inspired King James Bible can be found everywhere. Instead of securing it, if you "lukewarm" believe that every language has an inspired Bible, and if you believe that all English Bibles are equal in authority, you have not traveled far in your spiritual pilgrimage in Christ. Therefore, if you do not find the truth of the King James Bible, it is your fault. After all, finding God in Christ and the truth of the word of God is a premium.

CHAPTER 22

BORN UPSIDE DOWN

SURELY YOUR TURNING OF THINGS UPSIDE DOWN SHALL BE ESTEEMED AS THE POTTER'S CLAY...

ISAIAH 29:16

God is present in every detail of the ways of man. He is always speaking, teaching and warning. When a baby enters this world, he does so upside down. He does not enter feet first. This means that not only is man fallen, but he has fallen head first. God is speaking in this manner.

Because man is born upside down within as well, as indicated by his upside-down bodily entry, it becomes his accustomed way. He becomes very proficient at existing like this because the world is also upside down. This means that everything appears right side up even though it is not. The older a man becomes, the more hardened and convinced in this way he is. Because he was born this way, and the world matches him, he will always justify himself:

> *Woe unto them that call evil good, and good evil; That put darkness for light, and light for darkness; that put bitter for sweet, and sweet for bitter! Woe unto them that are wise in their own eyes, and prudent in their own sight! (Isa. 5:20,21)*

When you look around, you should picture all man-kind as standing on their heads for a better understanding of the way things are. This is why, in part, Jesus said, *"Ye must be born again (John 3:7)."*

When a man is born the second time, he is born feet first, as was the case of the Apostle Paul who was struck down on the road to Damascus:

> *And when we were all fallen to the earth, I heard a voice speaking unto me, and saying in the Hebrew tongue, Saul, Saul, why persecutest thou me? It is hard for thee to kick against the pricks. And I said, who art thou, Lord? And he said, I am Jesus whom thou persecutest. But arise and stand upon thy feet... ... (Acts 26:14-16)*

Paul had been walking around upside down on his head his whole life. Now he was persecuting those who held the truth of Jesus and "the way," thinking he was doing God service (John 16:2).

It is very easy with the power of the word of God to knock over people who are walking on their heads. This is what Jesus did to Paul, as the Word of God, he knocked him over. At the same moment, he was born again. Therefore, Jesus immediately commanded him, *"stand upon thy feet (Acts 26:16)."* For a second testimony, see Revelation 11:11 where the first sign of the entrance of the Spirit of life is to immediately stand on one's feet.

This is the case for everyone who is born again into the body of Christ. In the natural, when a child is born, it takes around a full year to be able to stand. However, the sons of God are born feet first and standing right side up. To the rest of the world who prolong head first living, the sons of God will be despised as upside down. Such is the nature of the flesh which is at enmity with the Spirit, *"Because the carnal mind is enmity against God... (Rom. 8:7)."*

Plainly speaking, the thought that God has not finished a specific Bible is an upside-down thought. The thought that God's original manuscripts are of greater value than His finished manuscripts is also an upside-down thought. Because *"the carnal mind is enmity against God (Rom. 8:7),"* there is a hostility from the start to the very thought that God has finished a Bible, especially the King James Bible as the very one.

The same Christians who say, "there cannot be only one Bible" are the same Christians who say, "there is only one way to heaven." The same Christians who say, "you must have the true Jesus (Word of God)" are the same Christians who say, "any Bible will do (word of God)." This too is upside-down-ness.

Study to shew thyself approved unto God, a workman that needeth not to be ashamed, rightly dividing the word of truth (2 Tim. 2:15)

Most churches will build every doctrine they hold, based on the Bible, except for their actual doctrine of the Bible itself. When asked about the nature of the Bible, they will not go to the word of God to explain, as is being expansively done in this book from start to finish.

If asked, "does your Bible contain mistakes? Translation errors? Where in your Bible does God show He is taking His hand off the Bible? How has the Bible come to us? Is one of them from God? Etc., etc.," what verses will they turn to for answers? Or will the conversation swerve to outside the Bible? Ideas "about" the Bible? History "about" the Bible? Natural thoughts "about" the Bible? Common sense "about" the Bible? All of these approaches are "outside" the Bible's self-revelation and none of these can be considered *"rightly dividing the word of truth (2 Tim. 2:15)."* To go outside the Bible and not seek its self-disclosure within its pages is an upside-down approach.

Above all, where has the idea come from that we must go back in time to ancient manuscripts to clarify what God's word is saying? And to which manuscripts is He telling us to go? The Textus Receptus manuscripts? The Alexandrian manuscripts? Who is to decide? Who told you that older manuscripts are better anyway? Etc., etc. If God Himself is not the one telling you this your search is upside-down.

This line of thinking has crept into the church and is now being handed down from generation to generation. Revelation has been traded for tradition in the name of human scholarship. Seminaries are being raised to solidify and perpetuate this false pretense and further the image of anti-Christ Bibles. This wholesale upside-down direction is being exalted and praised in our time as a great achievement:

Surely your turning of things upside down shall be esteemed as the potter's clay: For shall the work say of him that made it, He made me not? Or shall the thing framed say of him that framed it, He had no understanding? (Isa. 29:16)

Having achieved turning the doctrine of the nature of the Bible upside down and denouncing the King James Bible as the very word of God, the church is declaring to God, *"He had no understanding (vs. 16)."*

In our previous chapter, Jesus praised the queen of the South because she traveled North to Jerusalem to rectify her upside-down condition (Matt. 12:42). In the Bible, to go North indicates a right side up direction. She was not only seeking the truth about the person of Christ, as we saw that Solomon was a great type of, but the truth about the word of God as well, as we saw that Solomon wrote three of the books of the Bible. She went to the source for her answers:

To the law and to the testimony: If they speak not according to this word, It is because there is no light in them (Isa. 8:20)

If you cannot answer completely, and replete the matter of the doctrine of the scriptures, and their origin, nature, and development unto this day, by strictly being handed a Bible to do so, you may be at high risk as to how you hold them by faith. How then have you arrived at what you believe about the all-important Bible of our day if not from the Bible itself? Indeed, your faith may actually be found faith-less when judged by the word of God on *"the day (1 Cor. 3:13)."*

God is warning the church that she is upside down in the matter of the Bible. We will look at this closely after we have seen more of the stand-alone details of the King James Bible in chapters ahead.

CHAPTER 23

BOOKS

AND I SAW THE DEAD, SMALL AND GREAT, STAND BEFORE GOD; AND THE BOOKS WERE OPENED: AND ANOTHER BOOK WAS OPENED, WHICH IS THE BOOK OF LIFE: AND THE DEAD WERE JUDGED OUT OF THOSE THINGS WHICH WERE WRITTEN IN THE BOOKS, ACCORDING TO THEIR WORKS

REVELATION 20:12

The role that *"books (Rev. 20:12)"* are playing in the destiny of man cannot be over stated. Man's own earthly usage of books for recording and testifying is a reflection of God's way in heaven and is evidence that this dreadful day of judgement will come true.

The phrase *"book of life (Rev. 20:12)"* occurs "eight" times in the King James Bible representing Jesus, as was touched on in chapter twenty of this book as being common Bible knowledge. The *"book of life"* is therefore, *"the Lamb's book of life (Rev. 21:27)."*

The above side by side presence of *"the books (the Bible)"* and *"the Lamb's book of life (Jesus)"* at the great white throne judgment (Rev. 20:11), is the two-fold testimony of God (as covered in chapter 6 of this book) against all who *"stand before God (Rev. 20:12)"* at this judgment.

The *"books"* are the sixty-six books of the Bible *"and the dead were judged out of those things which were written in the books."* These are judged *"according to their works"* in light of the word of God: *"For all have sinned and come short of the glory of God (Rom. 3:23)."* These did not overcome by faith in God's finished work and have not their name's written in the *"book of life."*

The *"book of life,"* which is the *"Lamb's book of life,"* is actually the "Lamb" Himself, Jesus Christ. He is pictured in "book" terms because He is the Word of God and one with the Bible (as covered in chapters 4-6 of this book). This is made clear to us in the earlier part of the book of Revelation:

"He that overcometh… I will not blot his name out of the book of life, but I will confess his name before my Father… (Rev. 3:5)

In this verse we see that having one's name written in the *"book of life"* and Jesus confessing one's name is synonymous. Jesus' speaking out of Himself, the names of those who are in the *"book of life,"* is manifesting that He is this book that they are written in, *"I will confess his name."*

In our chapter header verse, both the Bible, the word of God, and Jesus, the Word of God, are present to condemn the guilty on this last day before the Father.

He that rejecteth me, and receiveth not my words, hath one that judgeth him: the word that I have spoken, the same shall judge him in the last day (John 12:48)

And…

But whosoever shall deny me before men, him will I also deny before my Father which is in heaven (Matt. 10:33)

Notice in the first verse how it is the Bible that judges, *"the word that I have spoken, the same shall judge him,"* and in the second verse it is Jesus who judges, *"him will I also deny."*

The hopelessness of this great white throne judgment day, where the Bible and Jesus Christ testify against all humanity who had not faith to enter into God's finished work, is the maturity of a "seed" first seen in the day of Moses:

> *And it came to pass, when Moses had made an end of writing the words of this law in a book, until they were finished, That Moses commanded the Levites, which bare the ark of the covenant of the Lord, saying, Take this book of the law, and put it in the side of the ark of the covenant of the Lord your God, that it may be there for a witness against thee (Deut. 31:24-26)*

In this Deuteronomy passage, the *"law (the Bible)"* and the *"ark (Jesus)"* are waiting together as a *"witness against"* the masses. Of course, the maturity of this seed comes in Revelation chapter twenty, as we have been reading.

This being so, we must not think that there is not a finished Bible prepared for this great day. God is very strict in His book keeping. The word "book(s)" appears exactly 196 times in the King James Bible. The words "Jesus Christ" also appear exactly 196 times in the King James Bible. This is deliberate in the KJV and exact to what we have thus seen about judgment day. If you are doubting this, please know that the words "son of man" also occur exactly 196 times in the King James Bible, as in, *"the Father... hath given him authority to execute judgment also, because he is the Son of man (John 5:26,27)."* Even the last occurrence of *"son of man"* appears in Revelation 14:14 (14 x 14 = 196). The books are straight.

So, let us examine the books. Our first natural question should be, "Did God select the books of the Bible?" At this point, most Christians would say, "Yes!" Indeed, there are no books missing from the Bible which should have been added, and there are no books included in the Bible which should have been left out.

In chapter nineteen of this book it was already stated and will be restated here, that the book of Isaiah contains sixty-six chapters which form a micro Bible, the Bible itself containing sixty-six books. The contents of each chapter of Isaiah match the contents of each book of the Bible in chronological order. This leaves no room for books to be missing or books to be wrongly included. If either were the case the whole body of the scriptures would not be fitly joined together and compacted but would be broken, and this cannot be (Eph. 4:16; John 10:35). For now, see Isaiah chapter forty and see the prophecy of John the Baptist, *"The voice of him that crieth in the wilderness, Prepare ye the way of the Lord, make straight in the desert a highway for our God (Isa. 40:3)."* The New Testament begins with the gospel of Matthew and is book number forty which matches Isaiah chapter forty. This is where we find the prophecy fulfilled in the coming of John the Baptist, *"For this is he that was spoken of by the prophet Esaias, saying, The voice of one crying in the wilderness, Prepare ye the way of the Lord, make his paths straight."* Again, we will be examining this specific "Isaiah 66 chapters/Bible 66 books" relationship in great detail toward the end of the book where we will run through each chapter/book match in consecutive order.

Rest assured that there are to be "exactly" and "only" sixty-six books in the Bible. Consecutively, the King James Bible speaks for itself:

For whatsoever things were written aforetime were written for our learning, that we through patience and comfort of the scriptures might have hope (Rom. 15:4)

In the above, the word of God tells us specifically that we are to take *"comfort in the scriptures."* The word *"comfort"* appears exactly sixty-six times in the King James Bible. That is one time for every book. The specific word *"comfort"* is rooted in the sixty-six books confirming its election and vice versa in the King James Bible.

Similar to the Romans 15:4 example is the book of Proverbs. The very first opening purpose statement verse for the book begins and ends with, *"To know wisdom… to perceive the words of understanding (Prov. 1:2)."*

Therefore, the word "wise" in the book of Proverbs appears exactly sixty-six times in the King James Bible. All forms of the word "know" and all forms of the word "understand" are also in the book of Proverbs exactly sixty-six times each in the King James Bible. Again, each of these word cases appears one time for every book in the Bible, confirming the Bible's total book count of sixty-six. In addition, reverse wise, this is telling you that the book of Proverbs belongs in the body of the King James Bible as one of the count of the sixty-six.

Knowing that God has selected the books of the Bible, this begs the next natural question, which is, "Did God select the order of the books of the Bible? To answer "No" is to say that God has departed from finishing the Bible at this early point.

The books of the Hebrew Bible (The Tanach) are in a different order than the finished Bible and have only twenty-four books total because they combine certain books together into one. This was inspired. And this was good for its time. This was the seed.

When the mature had come and the finished Bible was in the hands of the gentiles it too was inspired. And now the new order of the books was perfect for its time.

It was also perfect for its time that the cell division of the extra books took place. What was originally twenty-four books (combining: 1 and 2 Samuel; 1 and 2 Kings; 12 minor prophets; Ezra/Nehemiah; 1 and 2 Chronicles) had separated themselves to equal thirty-nine books in the Old Testament of the Bible. This was necessary since the New Testament was now come forth and the balance of the two was to be perfect.

For example, If the Old Testament books had not grown from twenty-four to thirty-nine, the total number of books in the Bible when adding the New Testament would be fifty-one and not sixty-six. This would not have been in harmony with the sixty-six chapters of Isaiah that are the micro Bible which we keep bringing up and will deeply cover again.

Another example, the book of Daniel, was originally the twenty-second book of the seed Hebrew Bible and became the twenty-seventh book of the Old Testament in the matured Bible. This was to match its counterpart book which is Revelation, which is the twenty-seventh book of the New Testament. If Daniel had not been moved to the twenty-seventh position it would have been out of place since Revelation, being last, could not be moved to match Daniel. This is the Bible's perfection.

Israel has never had a perfect Bible, meaning matured, meaning finished. Only the Gentiles have this, and it is only found in the King James Bible. All salvation matters, which include Jesus, the perfect Word of God and the King James Bible, the perfect word of God, are to strike jealousy in the heart of Israel:

I say then, have they stumbled that they should fall? God forbid: but rather through their fall salvation is come unto the gentiles, for to provoke them to jealousy (Rom. 11:11)

Not only should Israel be provoked *"to jealousy"* but if you are a gentile and have not cleaved to the King James Bible you should have jealousy in your heart over this perfect word of God which you lack believing on.

Other books of the Bible were in order from the beginning Hebrew seed and remain in the same order in the matured Bible. Their original placement was selected by God and selected to remain there. They would not move like the book of Daniel to meet the works of God, but rather, the works of God would manifest around them to complete their placement.

One example is the book of Leviticus which in both the Hebrew seed Bible and the matured King James Bible would be the third book of placement. Leviticus deals with the priestly order of the offerings, sacrifices and ordinances for dealing with sin. As such it could not be moved from the number "three" position. It is literally locked into place by threes: it deals with the "three" sins which are the lust of the flesh, the lust of the eyes and the pride of life, which entered in Genesis chapter "three;" Levi (Leviticus) was the "third" tribe (Gen. 29:34) of the "third" patriarch (Abraham, Isaac and Jacob, Ex. 3:6); Jesus petitioned the Father "three" times in the garden before fulfilling the book of Leviticus (Mark 14:41); Peter denied Jesus "three" times before the cock crow (Matt. 26:34); Jesus died between two malefactors, His own cross being the "third" (Luke 23:33); His Levitical death was at the "third" hour (Mark 15:25); His Levitical death was accompanied with "three" hours of darkness (Matt. 27:45); His Levitical death was accompanied by "three" Marys (John 19:25); His Levitical fulfilling of the offerings took him into the heart of the earth "three" days and "three" nights" (Matt. 12:40); Jesus after fulfilling the book of Leviticus rose from the dead on the "third" day according to the scriptures (1 Cor. 15:4). "According to the scriptures" includes all the "threes" He was surrounded with because "the book of Leviticus" was the "third" book. If all of these "threes" were not accompanying Jesus it would not have been "according to the scriptures."

The book of Leviticus did not move from book order number "three," or it would have been out of place with the issue of the maturity of the New Testament. However, within itself there was the furthering of growth. It reached a cellular division of twenty-seven chapters which is "three" x "three" x "three."

A second example, and a much more complex example, incorporates the shifting and rearranging of eight Old Testament books to match the doctrine of eschatology (end time doctrine) from the New Testament. The matured Bible lays out the following sequence of books, revealing God's intelligent new ordering of the books according to eschatology:

Ezra: In this book Israel repatriates into their land after being in Babylonian captivity. After 2,000 years of exile Israel is now geographically reoccupied by the nation.

Nehemiah: In this book Israel rebuilds their defense walls after repatriating with a sword in one hand and a trowel in the other. Israel has been, and will yet, build their defenses and the land.

Esther: This book begins with the gentile Queen Vashti being removed for disobedience to the word of the King. She was replaced immediately by a Jewish bride. Currently the gentile church is in place with the King of Kings. Her corporate decline in the word of God will coincide with the removal of the remnant in the rapture. Israel will immediately take the place of the church in world vision.

Job: This book is forty-two chapters of destruction in the life of a man who is targeted by the Devil. When Israel replaces the church on the world stage as God's focus, Israel will immediately enter forty-two months of God's final judgment upon them under the antichrist (Rev. 13:5).

Psalms: In this book David reveals the Messiah the Savior. Jesus, the true David will enter to save Israel from final extinction at the end of the forty-two-month judgment of antichrist (at the end of the forty-two chapters of Job).

Proverbs: This book is about knowledge, wisdom and understanding. After the true David enters to save Israel the thousand-year millennium will begin of Jesus Christ, *"the government shall be upon his shoulder: and his name shall be called Wonderful, Counselor… (Isa. 9:6)."*

Ecclesiastes: In this book there is nothing new under the sun and all things repeat themselves. After the thousand-year reign of the Prince of Peace, Jesus Christ, the Devil is released for one more time and a final purging takes place.

Song of Solomon: In this book is captured the love affair of all love affairs. After the Devil and the great white throne judgment of the damned comes the eternal and unending love affair of Christ and the bride of Christ.

Isaiah: In this book is the sixty-six micro books of the Bible, the eternal word of God. In the eternal, the bride of Christ will reveal the unending glorious works of the eternal word of God, the Bible, she believed on.

With each chapter of this book we are stepping closer to helping the believer to have faith in the perfect work of Christ in the KJV. For many, they will stand at the judgment like a nightmare come true and the worst of realities will hit them. They will see Jesus standing there and the King James Bible ready to testify against them. Having denied that Jesus is real and having denied that the King James Bible is the actual word of God, both will now sentence them to a Christ-less eternity in the lake of fire for denying them as the truth (Rev. 20:15).

Now, while it is still today, we must raise our low view of the Bible in general, to a high view of the Bible in His finished word, the King James Bible. By beginning wide with the topic of "books" in this chapter, we have begun to taste just a little of the perfection of the word of God. We will tighten the scope to "chapters" then "verses" then "words" then "letters" then "numbers" in the chapters ahead. This will take us further yet into faith and bring us into rest in the finished word of God that we may believe on Him. This book is for leading people in the finished work of Christ (KJV).

I would be remiss not to make special mention at the end of this chapter and each of the following chapters on the subject of "chapters, verses, words, letters, numbers," that any examples are merely an insignificant amount of the incredible whole. The scope of this book is not to exhaust every perfect work of God in His finished Bible, the King James Bible, but to serve the believer to believe yet and the unbeliever to stumble further.

CHAPTER 24

CHAPTERS

THY WORD IS TRUE FROM THE BEGINNING: AND EVERY ONE OF THY RIGHTEOUS JUDGMENTS ENDURETH FOREVER

PSALM 119:160

God's word *"endureth forever"* because it is *"true from the beginning (Ps. 119:60)."* Similar speech would be to say that God's word is finished upon delivery into the world because it is already *"finished from the foundation of the world (Heb. 4:3)."* In the simplest of words (but deepest of thought), that which already "is" in eternity "manifests so" in time. Despite appearance otherwise, man has made no contribution or interference from his "self" to the completion (manifestation) of the Bible.

Christ has come into the world the same way. Man has made no contribution or interference from his "self" to the perfection (manifestation) of Jesus. He is *"the Lamb slain from the foundation of the world (Rev. 13:8)."*

The Father has done it all:

And if thou wilt make me an altar of stone, thou shalt not build it of hewn stone: for if thou lift up thy tool upon it, thou hast polluted it (Ex. 20:25)

Those were the instructions God gave Moses. For man to *"lift up thy tool"* is to engage the "self" in the work of cutting the *"stone"* that only God can cut and has already cut.

Moses passed on God's instructions to Joshua when it came time to pass on the role of leadership and enter the promised land. This instruction was revealing Jesus and the Bible in the stones formed exclusively by God:

And there shalt thou build an altar unto the Lord thy God, an altar of stones: thou shalt not lift up any iron tool upon them... whole stones... and thou shalt offer burnt offerings thereon... and thou shalt write upon the stones all the words of this law very plainly (Deut. 27:5-8)

The usage of the stone altar for *"burnt offerings"* typifies Jesus upon the altar of the cross. The Bible is also clearly typified in *"write upon the stones all the words of this law."* These stones were ordered to be *"whole stones"* which indicates that the work was already *"finished from the foundation of the world (Heb. 4:3)"* by God.

Joshua thoroughly obeyed this command consciously (Josh. 8:30-32). David the shepherd boy obeyed subconsciously when he slew Goliath the giant with his sling:

And he took his staff in his hand, and chose him five smooth stones out of the brook, and put them in a shepherd's bag which he had, even in a scrip (1 Sam. 17:40)

These *"smooth stones"* had been formed by God and not man. David put the stones in a *"scrip"* which means *"a shepherd's bag."* However, at the same time, *"scrip"* is a short version of "scripture." Do not think this chosen translational English word in the King James Bible, to express the original Hebrew word, was unintentional by God. This language work is called a double entendre and is a quality of the matured Bible peaking with revelation knowledge. Again, we see the God formed *"stone"* work of Jesus and the Bible *"scrip*-ture" matched together.

When Daniel the prophet reveals and interprets King Nebuchadnezzar's spirit troubling dream, he states that beginning with his own kingdom of gold, the kingdoms of world history of silver and brass and iron and clay, will all be lined up to be smote, destroyed, broken in pieces and consumed. This would be executed by a "stone cut out without hands (Dan. 2:34)."

Forasmuch as thou sawest that the stone was cut out of the mountain without hands, and that it brake in pieces the iron, the brass, the clay, the silver, and the gold; the great God hath made known to the king what shall come to pass hereafter: and the dream is certain, and the interpretation thereof sure (Dan. 2:45)

Daniel and King Nebuchadnezzar were seeing first glimpse of the apocalyptic return of Jesus Christ in Revelation chapter nineteen of the Bible. The spiritual quality of Jesus Christ is "the stone cut out without hands." No man has made contribution or interference from the "self" to His perfection. This description also applies to the Bible, which takes us back to chapter six of this book where Jesus fulfills Daniel 2:45 and is described this way at His violent return: *"And he was clothed with a vesture dipped in blood: and his name is called The Word of God (Rev. 19:13)."* No man has made contribution or interference from the "self" to the completion of the Bible either.

Throughout this book we have been letting scripture divide scripture and then walking in the divide. The only perfect way to interpret the Bible is to follow God, *"follow me (Matt. 19:21),"* in the divided path He has cut in His word by His own hand. God is always "dividing" the way for His people to follow Him and never relying on their "self" for this. Think of the crossing of the Red Sea in the Exodus from Egypt (Ex. 14:21). Think of the crossing of the River Jordan for the promise land conquest (Josh. 3:13). Think of the body of Jesus for entering the presence of God (Mark 15:38/Heb. 10:20). These are but a few examples of God dividing and His people following.

It is very easy to see the first divide of the Bible that God has cut and to strictly trust Him and follow in it: The Old Testament and the New

Testament. Think of the dividing of the sheep on the right and the goats on the left (Matt. 25:32). God divided the Old Testament from the New Testament in the Bible. No man contributed from his "self" to divide the Bible in this way.

It is still very easy to trust and follow God further into His dividing the Bible. In the last chapter of this book we saw that God divided the books written by the Spirit, out of the world and into the Bible. He also divided the books that were not written by the Spirit, out of the Bible and back into the world where they came from (the apocrypha). This left sixty-six books exactly. These books were divided into an order from Genesis to Revelation. No man contributed from his "self" to develop this inclusion and formation of the sixty-six books of the Bible. God alone divided these by the leading of His Holy Spirit.

To go by faith further into God's dividing of the Bible might not be as easy for you. Knowing that God has divided the Old Testament from the New Testament and within those He has divided all the books of the Bible, the next natural question is begged, which is, "Did God divide the chapters of the books of the Bible?" To answer "No" here, is to say that God has departed at this junction from finishing the Bible Himself and left it to be *"hewn"* and *"polluted (Ex. 20:25)"* by men out of their "self."

Not so. God's way is to do the dividing Himself. All of it. This is why He speaks with words such as these in the King James Bible, *"a time, and times, and half a time (Rev. 12:14)"* and *"Six hundred threescore and six (Rev. 13:18)."* These are just a couple examples of expressing something using terms of division rather than "three and a half years (Rev. 12:14)" or "666 (Rev. 13:18)." God wants you to know that He will do the dividing and you will do the following.

Let's follow Jesus who is always *"rightly dividing the word of truth (2 Tim. 2:15)"* for us in the King James Bible and see His perfection uniquely on display in the "chapters."

Solomon who typified Christ, as we put forth in chapter twenty-one of this book, was oft bringing forth Christ, whether he knew it or not. He said this, *"Which yet my soul seeketh, but I find not: one man among a thousand have I found; but a woman among all those have I not found (Ecc. 7:28)."*

Of course, there was no way for him to know that John chapter three would be the one thousandth chapter of the finished Bible where the *"one man among a thousand"* would be most famously recognized, *"For God so loved the world, that he gave his only begotten Son, that whosoever believeth in him should not perish, but have everlasting life (John 3:16)."*

While we are recognizing John chapter three as the one-thousandth chapter of the Bible, we must recognize it as the beginning chapter of teaching regarding the kingdom of God, *"Jesus answered and said unto him, Verily, verily, I say unto thee, Except a man be born again, he cannot see the kingdom of God (John 3:3),"* and *"Jesus answered, Verily, verily I say unto thee, Except a man be born of water and of the Spirit, he cannot enter into the kingdom of God (John 3:5)."* We must make note that the *"kingdom of God"* is a one-thousand-year reign of Jesus Christ (Rev. 20:2,3,4,5,6,7), matching the one thousandth chapter of the Bible where we are instructed how to enter into it, "John 3."

The more you come to know the word of God, the more you will come to know that it is all about glorifying Jesus Christ for the pleasure of the Father. There are creatures living in the depths of the sea that no man knows are there, but they are there for glorifying Jesus Christ for the pleasure of the Father, whether man knows of them or not. Likewise, the King James Bible is thick and through with knowledge that glorifies Jesus Christ for the pleasure of the Father, that most men will never know is there. Did you know that God rains down bread from heaven to feed the children of Israel in the wilderness in Exodus chapter sixteen? *"Then said the Lord unto Moses, Behold, I will rain bread from heaven for you (Ex. 16:4)."* Did you know that Exodus sixteen is the sixty-sixth chapter of the Old Testament? Not only is the bread that comes down from heaven speaking of Jesus as the bread of life (John 6:33-35), but it is speaking of the "sixty-six books of the Bible" as the bread of life as well (Deut. 8:3). Did you know that Jesus breaks bread with His disciples on the night of His death in Luke chapter twenty-two? *"Now the feast of unleavened bread drew nigh... then came the day of unleavened bread... and he took bread, and gave thanks, and brake it, and gave unto them, saying, This is my body which is given for you... (Luke 22:1,7,19)."* Did you know that Luke twenty-two is the sixty-sixth chapter of the New Testament? Not only is the unleavened bread that Jesus is breaking (dividing), speaking of the sinlessness of Jesus, but it is speaking of the perfect "sixty-six books of the Bible" as unpolluted by man as well. You may not know these things are there in the finished Bible. The finished Bible may not be for you, but it is always for God in the enjoyment of His Son.

Particularly, the Father enjoys the Son as the "sweet savour" of the sacrifices He fulfilled in the offerings upon the altar for the redemption of the souls of men. We covered this in the last chapter where Jesus was surrounded by "threes" as the great high priest of Leviticus dying for the sin of the world. Remember how there are twenty-seven chapters in Leviticus in order for the count to be 3 x 3 x 3? This was an example of chapters "rightly divided (2 Tim. 2:15)." We are to follow God in this revelation for thick and through understanding that *"Christ died for our sins according to the scriptures (1 Cor. 15:3)."* The phrase of the Father, "sweet savour," appears in six books of the Bible. Six is the number of man. The phrase "sweet savour" appears in those six books in a total of eighteen chapters, which is 6 + 6 + 6, or the infamous "666" which is the intensified number of man in his deepest depravity, even antichrist. The Father's "sweet savour" is Jesus, the sacrifice for these sinners. Do you remember that we have mentioned the common knowledge of the number eight is the number for Jesus? The phrase "sweet savour" is first mentioned in the eighth chapter of the Old Testament. The phrase "sweet savour" appears over and over and over in the Old Testament and then only one final time alone in the New Testament in 2 Corinthians, which is the eighth book of the New Testament. The "sweet savour" of the Father is marked by the number six in that it is for man's sake and the number eight in that it is Jesus alone from beginning to end.

Do you remember that man is upside down as was covered in chapter twenty-two of this book? Since we have brought up antichrist, did you know that going "backwards" in the Bible, the 666'th chapter is Psalm

46? Did you know that the famous verse, *"Be still, and know that I am God (Ps. 46:10)"* is in this chapter? Did you know that while this verse belongs to God, this chapter is also a picture of antichrist, who being that man of sin *"opposeth and exalteth himself above all that is called God, or that is worshipped; so that he as God sitteth in the temple of God, shewing himself that he is God (2 Thess. 2:4)"*? Do you remember that in chapter fourteen of this book it is said that William Shakespeare was in the service of King James court? Did you know that in this chapter forty-six of Psalms, the forty-sixth word is *"shake"* and that the forty-sixth word from the end of the verse text is *"spear"* and that Shakespeare's age is approximated to be forty-six during the completion of the King James Bible? Do not think that Shakespeare manipulated this into the text. That would have required the Hebrew words for "shake" and "spear" of Psalm forty-six long ago to have been manipulated to be in the exact chapter in the exact place in the verses. It also would require that Shakespeare was born exactly when he was born. This is only by the work of the Spirit to show you antichrist and demonstrate antichrist's way even as it says in Jude four, *"For there are certain men crept in unawares, who were before of old ordained to this condemnation..."* Shakespeare is placing himself in the seat of God in this chapter.

Once we begin the level of "chapters" we begin to do a lot of counting. Since we have brought up 666, let's examine its surrounding instructions, *"Here is wisdom. Let him that hath understanding count the number of the beast: for it is the number of a man; and his number is Six hundred threescore and six (Rev. 13:18)."* God has advised us that there is *"wisdom"* and *"understanding"* in the counting of His word. There is only one other verse in the entire Bible where we are given a second witness and confirmation that God desires us to count His word, and it comes to us out of the *"wisdom"* and *"understanding"* of Solomon again, *"Behold, this have I found, saith the preacher, counting one by one, to find out the account (Ecc. 7:27)."* Did you know that this chapter in Ecclesiastes is the 666'th chapter in the King James Bible? Yes, the only two chapters that tell us to count, both have a direct relationship of expression of six-hundred-sixty-six.

On the opposite end of the book of Revelation is the book of Genesis where the generation of Adam is laid out telling us he lived 930 years. In the middle section is the gospel of Matthew where in chapter one is the generation of Jesus Christ. Matthew chapter one is the 930'th chapter of the Bible. Did you know that the life of Christ is for taking over after your Adamic life expires? This is a very consequential revelation.

God is always counting, and all things are counted and numbered by Him and there is nothing that is, that He has not measured according to its exact number. The chapters of the Bible are no different and each is in its proper division by Him. Even passages that seem inconsequential must have their divine order:

"Now the children of Israel after their number, to wit, the chief fathers and captains of thousands and hundreds, and their officers that served the king in any matter of the courses, which came in and went out month by month throughout all the months of the year, of every course were twenty and four thousand (1 Chronicles 27:1)

Such verses seem so uneventful. Yet, did you know that according to as it is written *"month by month throughout all the months of the year"* in this verse, it is there because this verse begins the three-hundred-sixty-fifth chapter of the Bible? Yes, this is the 365'th chapter of the Bible according to the 365 days of the year. Do not say that the Jewish calendar differs in days. The finished Bible of God, the King James Bible, was granted stewardship into the hands of the gentiles.

Through counting, God has made His Bible easy to memorize passage locations. We saw in the last chapter of this book that the twenty-seventh book of the Old Testament is Daniel which matches its New Testament counterpart which is the twenty-seventh book of Revelation. Daniel chapter 12 has matching content to Revelation chapter 12 (See Dan. 12:1/Rev. 12:7 and see Dan. 12:6/Rev. 12:6 for sampling). Deuteronomy chapter 13 is the seed chapter which is devoted to the description of false prophets, Ezekiel chapter 13 is devoted to growth description of false prophets, Acts chapter 13, "Bar-jesus," is called a "false prophet" by name, and Revelation chapter 13 is devoted to the maturity of description of the ultimate false prophet who will make the way for the beast. Immediately following is Revelation chapter "14" where, in verse "14:4," is described the "144,000" who received not the mark of the beast in their foreheads but the Father's name instead. Genesis chapter 19 has matching content to Judges chapter 19 (See Gen. 19:4-11/Judges 19:22-25). Zechariah chapter 6 reveals the four horses of the Apocalypse which mature in Revelation chapter 6. Matthew chapter 25 is three parables of twenty-five: the parable of the virgins, five wise and five foolish, which is 5 x 5 = 25; The parable of the talents, five were given to a man and he traded to get five more, which is 5 x 5 = 25; and the parable of the dividing of the nations, the sheep on his right hand and the goats on his left hand. Each hand has five fingers, which is 5 x 5 = 25. And so on, and so on it goes.

You may not have known all of this, but God does:

The words of the Lord are pure words: as silver tried in a furnace of earth, purified seven times (Psalm 12:6)

King James gave strict orders to the translator committee of the King James Bible. Article number fourteen of the rules of engagement for the translating of the King James Bible was: *These translations to be used when they agree better with the text than the Bishop's Bible, viz. Tyndale's, Coverdale's, Matthew's, Wilchurch's, Geneva (By "Wilchurch" is meant the Great Bible, which was printed by Edward Wilchurch, one of King Henry VIII's printers).* This was the spreading vine of the growing word of God that reached through history and matured into the King James Version.

This *"vine (John 15:5)"* of Bible translations into English that were the growth and issue of the King James Bible, numbered six, making the King James Bible the final translation as the seventh, according to Psalm 12:6, *"purified seven times."* Psalm 12 is the 490'th chapter of the Bible, which is 7+7+7+7+7+7+7+7+7+7+7+7+7+7+7+7+7+7+7+7+7+7+7+7+7+7+7+7+7+7+ 7+7+7+7+7+7+7+7+7+7+7+7+7+7+7+7+7+7+7+7+7+7+7+7+7+7+7+7+7+7+ 7+7+7+7 = 490'th chapter. Common Bible knowledge will testify that "7" is God's number for spiritual completion. Chapter for chapter, the King

James Bible is God's spiritually completed Bible as the *"fruit"* of the *"vine (John 15:5)."*

I close this chapter reminding the reader that these examples are the insignificant amount of the whole regarding God's dividing of the chapters in the King James Bible. Again, the scope of this book does not allow exhaustive demonstration but serves to give sight to the blind, and blind those who say they see (John 9:39).

CHAPTER 25

VERSES

SEEK YE OUT THE BOOK OF THE LORD,
AND READ: NO ONE OF THESE SHALL
FAIL, NONE SHALL WANT HER MATE: FOR
MY MOUTH IT HATH COMMANDED, AND
HIS SPIRIT IT HATH GATHERED THEM

ISAIAH 34:16

When Jesus, the Word of God made flesh, came into the world, He ministered with miracles, wonders and signs: *"Ye men of Israel, hear these words; Jesus of Nazareth, a man approved of God among you by miracles and wonders and signs, which God did by him in the midst of you, as you yourselves also know (Acts 2:22)."* In fact, as stated in this verse, Jesus was publicly being *"approved of God"* by these.

God has likewise been ministering miracles, wonders and signs in the King James Bible to the world in real life and in real time for over four-hundred years. These miracles, signs, and wonders, are God's public approval to all men as to which Bible is sourced and finished of him. We have been seeing many of these miracles, wonders, and signs, and they are literally unending beyond what will be shared in this book. Surely, at the last day, God will be making His boast to the world of unbelievers by His Son and by His word, the Bible. Be reminded of this verse we covered on "Books" in chapter twenty-three: *"He that rejecteth me, and receiveth not my words, hath one that judgeth him: the word that I have spoken, the same shall judge him in the last day (John 12:48)."*

You may think it is unimportant to believe that God has finished a Bible. Apart from the risk of standing exposed as an unbeliever, to your own surprise, at the *"last day (John 12:48),"* have you considered the following?

Are you not trusting God to finish the work of salvation in you that He began (Phil. 1:6)? Doesn't He need to gather every detail related to this in your life, bring it to pass, and bring it to a matured completion?

And are you not trusting the Lord to keep track of your corrupted, dishonorable and weak body which is being sown into the earth, to gather it all and raise it up entirely in incorruption, glory, power and immortality into a spiritual body at the resurrection (1 Cor. 15:42-44)?

And when Enoch was translated from this world, not seeing death, and gathered unto the Lord, needn't he trust that God would make this complete and perfect (Heb. 11:5)? And when Philip was caught away after baptizing the Ethiopian eunuch, needn't he trust that the Lord would gather him complete and perfect for this relocating (Acts 8:39,40)? And should you, the last days believer, be caught up to meet the Lord in the air, are you not trusting the Lord to gather you correctly, entirely and in perfection (1 Thess. 4:17)?

Here is the case and point for all of these "gatherings" listed above: *"My mouth it hath commanded, and his Spirit it hath gathered them (Isa. 34:16)."* In other words, God Himself has done it. You can trust Him to do them all completely, correctly, entirely and perfectly.

All of these "gatherings" are also cases of "translation." To translate means to change something's location or its form or its condition or even its nature. It means to take something from one state and gather it into a new state. God uses the word "translate" one time and the word "translated" two times in the King James Bible. In each and every case of the three usages of the words, it is taking something inferior and translating it into a superior condition. The kingdom was translated from Saul to David (2 Sam. 3:10). Enoch was translated from this world to the next (Heb. 11:5). And the church has been translated from the power of darkness into the kingdom of God's dear Son (Col. 1:13). These are all superior translations of God. This is also the case for God's finished Bible in the King James version, it has taken the Hebrew and Greek and a little Aramaic and translated them into a superior English Bible for God's glory. Recall this verse which came up in chapter five of this book: *"truth: for thou hast magnified thy word above all thy name (Ps. 138:2)."*

We have thus seen that the books of the Bible have all been selected by God. They have all been ordered by God. And God has divided the chapters. The books, the order and the chapters all have to do with His "gathering" to which He says, *"No one of these shall fail, none shall want her mate (Isa. 34:16)."* We must know that this "gathering" of the whole is nothing without its parts. So, we rhetorically ask, "Are all the verses of the Bible gathered and placed and numbered by God as well?" To answer "No" here is to discredit the word of God which shows otherwise on every page. It also means you believe God has departed the raising of His word, the Bible, at this incomplete place, and the glory of these miracles, wonders and signs belong to another.

You must shun any such idea that the verses in the bible just happen to be where they are as if through wandering they have just ended up being there. Cain was a wanderer. When he went out from the presence of the Lord, he dwelt in the land of Nod, on the East of Eden (Gen. 4:16). The name "Nod" means "to wander." Cain's father, Satan, was also a wanderer. He goes to and fro and up and down in the earth (Job 2:2). In fact, all those who follow Satan, God calls wanderers in the King James Bible (Jude 13).

No! God has meticulously placed all the verses in the mature King James Bible, and done so as for each to have a *"mate (Isa. 34:16)."* Beginning with the judgment of the chief wanderer himself, here is a very simple example of a verse and its mate:

And the Lord God said unto the serpent, Because thou hast done this, thou art cursed above all cattle, and above every beast of the field; upon thy belly shalt thou go, and dust shalt thou eat all the days of thy life (Gen. 3:14)

Genesis 3:14 is the commencing verse of the judgment of Satan in the Old Testament. We see its New Testament ratification in John 3:14 because these verses are mated together. In John 3:14 Jesus is re-instructing Nicodemus back to the commencing verse of the original judgment of the serpent in Genesis 3:14…

And as Moses lifted up the serpent in the wilderness, even so must the Son of man be lifted up (John 3:14)

Once illuminated to things like the above match "Gen. 3:14/John 3:14," verses and their mates will begin to manifest everywhere in your opening of the King James Bible. Here is an example of a flock of verses, first in Matthew, then in Mark, then in Luke:

And every one that hath forsaken houses, or brethren, or sisters, or father, or mother, or wife, or children, or lands, for my name's sake, shall receive an hundredfold, and shall inherit everlasting life. But many that are first shall be last; and the last shall be first (Matthew 19:29,30)

And Jesus answered and said, Verily I say unto you, There is no man that hath left house, or brethren, or sisters, or father, or mother, or wife, or children, or lands, for my sake, and the gospel's, But he shall receive an hundredfold now in this time, houses, and brethren, and sisters, and mothers, and in the world to come eternal life (Mark 10:29,30)

And he said unto them, Verily I say unto you, There is no man that hath left house, or parents, or brethren, or wife, or children, for the kingdom of God's sake, Who shall not receive manifold more in this present time, and in the world to come life everlasting (Luke 18:29,30)

All three of these clusters have rooted themselves in the verse 29,30 position. Do not think that this a synoptic gospel copying issue. These three are mates. Matthew's verses 29,30 come at the end of the chapter.

Mark's verses 29,30 come in a chapter which continues up to fifty-two verses. And Luke's verses 29,30 come in a chapter of forty-three total verses. None the less, these verses would not wander out of place in their chapter, but all have halted themselves in the 29,30 verse positions to set together. The subject matter of these verses is very appropriate for a verse 30 anchoring, since that was the age that Jesus Himself left house, brethren, sisters, mother, opportunity for wife and all, for the gospel and for the kingdom (Luke 3:23). Amen.

If you do not believe that these verses were set by God in the King James Bible like diamonds, consider the following example from the New Testament again:

Knowing this, that our old man is crucified with him, that the body of sin might be destroyed, that henceforth we should not serve sin (Rom. 6:6)

We have nailed it down before that "six" is the number of man, as man was created on the "sixth" day. The word *"man"* in this verse is the "sixth" word of the "sixth" verse of the "sixth" chapter of the "sixth" book of the New Testament in the King James Bible. This too is mating.

Entire chapters can be mated as well. Going back into the Old Testament, let's look at Psalm 100:3 which is a very famous scripture:

Know ye that the Lord he is God: it is he that hath made us, and not we ourselves; we are his people, and the sheep of his pasture (Psalm 100:3)

Psalm 100 has a total verse count of 1 through 5 with this famous *"sheep"* scripture being in verse 3. These specifics mate it to the most famous "100 sheep" verse in the New Testament which begins in Luke 15 and verse 3 where Jesus tells the parable of the lost sheep...

And he spake this parable unto them saying, What man among you, having an hundred sheep, if he loses one of them... ... (Luke 15:3ff)

These *"mates"* share the "100 sheep" and the "1" and the "5" and the "3" for infra structure, strength, continuity, relationship, symmetry, emphasis, value, beauty, prestige, perfection: Psalm 100:1-5 in verse 3 mated to 100 sheep in Luke 15 verse 3.

God's field of vision is not limited like ours. Man has straight forward vision with a very small amount of peripheral vision. When we read the Bible, we only see one single word of one single verse in focus at a time. That verse is surrounded by other verses, in a chapter that is surrounded by other chapters, that is in a book surrounded by other books, making up the Bible. God's vision is everywhere. It sees the entire Bible in dimensional focus all at once. It must be perfect in His sight from every angle and from every perspective and it must glorify Him by adorning the doctrine of God at every depth of examination.

The total number of verses in the Old Testament is adorning the doctrine of God. The total number of verses in the old testament is 23145 verses in the KJV. What looks like a random number of verses, or a handful of numbers, can be immediately seen doctrinally for what they are. If we use our eyes to organize these numbers, we have 12345. Even running in the background of the King James Bible is the Old Testament truth that God is counting. The Old Testament in a word is about the law, and the law is all about God counting: Counting your sins; counting your trespasses; counting your days; counting your judgment. God is running doctrinal reinforcement in the finished Bible underlining the clear revelation of the word of God that the count will be against you if you approach Him by the measure of the law, *"But that no man is justified by the law in the sight of God, it is evident: for, The just shall live by faith (Gal. 3:11)."*

God is spectacular everywhere we turn. His works are staggering to us, and His acts are limitless:

He telleth the number of the stars; he calleth them all by their names. Great is our Lord, and of great power: his understanding is infinite (Ps. 147:4,5)

Christian reader, do you really believe that God has numbered the stars and calls them each and every by their name? It is unthinkable and unconscionable to believe that God has done this with the stars that fall from the sky, but as for the verses of the precious Bible which shall never pass away He has not. Every verse is accounted for and is in its proper place and has its own name. The verse, *"I can do all things through Christ which strengtheneth me"* has a name, and that name is *"Philippians 4:13."* The verse, *"Trust in the Lord with all thine heart; and lean not unto thine own understanding"* has a name, and that name is *"Proverbs 3:5."* The verse *"For I know the thoughts that I think toward you…"* has a name, and that name is *"Jeremiah 29:11."* The verse, *"I am my beloved's and my beloved is mine…"* is named *"Song of Solomon 6:3." "Put on the whole armour of God…"* is named *"Ephesians 6:11." "No weapon that is formed against thee shall prosper…"* is named *"Isa. 54:17." "Have not I commanded thee? Be strong and of a good courage…"* is named *"Joshua 1:9." "The Lord is my shepherd; I shall not want"* is named *"Psalm 23.1."* These are all very famous verses and names. To say you know the verse but not the address is comparable to saying, "I recognize your face, but I can't remember your name." To think that mere men have assigned divisions and reference numbers to the Bible for incidental handiness and not acknowledge that God has placed and named all His verses, is far, far, away, from trembling at His word: *"Hear the word of the Lord, ye that tremble at his word,"* and the name is *"Isaiah 66:5."*

Just like stars, the verses are numbered. And just like stars, the verses are named. And just like stars, the verses are all differing in glory, *"for one star differeth from another star in glory (1 Cor. 15:41)."* The above cited verses being all famous in glory, at the end of the last chapter we cited a not so famous verse, which by name be *"1 Chronicles 27:1."* We said that despite its mundane appearance and seeming insignificance it had need to be called into divine order. We said, by its proper placement in the 365'th chapter of the Bible this verse matched its quotation as it is written *"month by month throughout all the months of the year."* Let's look at it and close another chapter with it again:

> *"Now the children of Israel after their number, to wit, the chief fathers and captains of thousands and hundreds, and their officers that served the king in any matter of the courses, which came in and went out month by month throughout all the months of the year, of every course were twenty and four thousand (1 Chronicles 27:1)*

Beyond being in the proper chapter, as a standalone verse this is verse number 11111 bearing the relationship to its content *"thousands and hundreds."* Although this verse lacks an outward sense of greatness like other famous verses, it is full of the glory of the Lord, even a double portion, if we would just take our time to get to know it in the King James Bible. In this way, the body of the Bible is again exactly designed like the human body, and like the body of Christ, giving higher decoration to the less striking parts for the sake of the overall balance of beauty of the whole:

And those members of the body, which we think to be less honourable, upon these we bestow more abundant honour; and our uncomely parts have more abundant comeliness. For our comely parts have no need: but God hath tempered the body together, having given more abundant honour to that part which lacked (1 Cor. 12:23,24)

We again close chapter with the reminder that our sampled verses are a mere token of the vastness of remarkable verses in the finished King James Bible. Again, the scope of this book is only to illuminate you to this truth that you may believe, God willing.

CHAPTER 26

WORDS

>SURELY MEN OF LOW DEGREE ARE
>VANITY, AND MEN OF HIGH DEGREE ARE
>A LIE: TO BE LAID IN THE BALANCE, THEY
>ARE ALTOGETHER LIGHTER THAN VANITY
>
>PSALM 62:9

I greatly fear for the man who is telling God's people that the King James Bible is not the very word of God. Such a man is under the seduction of the *"spirit of the world (1 Cor. 2:12)."*

I fear greater yet for the man who has made a career, a so-called ministry, out of tearing down the King James Bible as the very word of God by exalting his own mind, out of the self.

In world culture, we associate *"men of high degree,"* such as have "Master of Divinity" and "Doctor of Theology," as those who know God well. However, if these men knew God well, they would know that God's position is: *"men of high degree are a lie... they are altogether lighter than vanity (Ps. 62:9)."* And if these men knew God well, they would resist this temptation of the world in order to escape this condemnation of God. And if these men knew God well, they would not perpetuate this condemnation to the next generation.

The Lord Jesus Christ denied this temptation and escaped this condemnation for Himself and all His generation who would be born again of Him: *"Can the blind lead the blind? Shall they both not fall into the ditch? The disciple is not above his master: but everyone that is perfect shall be as his master (Luke 6:39,40)."* Instead of perfecting following the master, the church is perfecting the *"lie."*

This *"lie"* of achievement in the academic system for the earning of a degree for the equating of knowing God well, is old and will always carry the end result of changing God's "words" in the finished Bible today. Remember, in chapter three of this book, "Satan, The Self, And The KJV," we saw that both Satan and Eve changed God's words. This was the seed of old.

This seed of old of changing God's "words" grew in *"men of high degree"* in the day of Jesus. Remember, in chapter fourteen of this book, "Man, The Cross, And The KJV," we saw that above the head of Jesus, upon the cross, was scripture by inspiration of God, *"JESUS OF NAZARETH THE KING OF THE JEWS (John 19:19)."* Pilate had written word for word out of the mouth of God, but the chief priests of the Jews would not receive its wording from God, and demanded it be changed:

> *Then said the chief priests of the Jews to Pilate, Write not, The King of the Jews; but that he said, I am King of the Jews (John 19:21)*

Pilate's response to them was also straight out of the mouth of God:

> *Pilate answered, What I have written I have written (vs. 22)*

Today we are seeing the maturity of this seed which was planted in the garden, and was growing in the day of Jesus, as men continue to disregard the revelation and self-disclosure of the finished Bible, the King James Bible. Today more than ever, men are cloaking themselves in degrees and associating themselves with prestigious names of schools and teachers. The end result cannot differ from the seed, and that seed is to change the "words" of God. Therefore, you will inevitably be strongly told by these influential men that the King James Bible is mistaken, is mistranslated, and is not the authoritative word of God, His finished Bible. They will then refer you to another translation, even all translations. If you resist and stand firm that God has finished a Bible, the King James Bible, they will kill you in one way or another.

But what God has written God has written. There is more at stake to there being a finished Bible than we will ever know on this side of eternity. This means there is more at stake to our believing on the finished Bible than we will ever know on this side of eternity. When Jesus stood for a finished Bible they immediately sought to kill Him. Not only did Jesus stand for a finished Bible but it was the King James Bible that He was standing for, according to Luke:

And there was delivered unto him the book of the prophet Esaias. And when he had opened the book, he found the place where it was written, The Spirit of the Lord is upon me, because he hath anointed me to preach the gospel to the poor; he hath sent me to heal the brokenhearted, to preach deliverance to the captives, and recovering of sight to the blind, to set at liberty them that are bruised, To preach the acceptable year of the Lord. And he closed the book, and he gave it again to the minister, and sat down. And the eyes of all them that were in the synagogue were fastened on him. And he began to say unto them, this day is the scripture fulfilled in your ears (Luke 4:17-21)

In every way in this versing, just as we have seen in our previous sections titled "Books, Chapters, Verses," the finished King James Bible is presented to us by the Spirit according to Luke.

In verse seventeen it is written, *"And there was delivered unto him the book of the prophet Esais."* As we continue to reference, the book of Isaiah is the micro Bible with sixty-six chapters matching the sixty-six books of the Bible in chronological order by content (to be explored at this book's end). Jesus was here holding the seed of the entire finished Bible in His hands, as was covered in depth in chapter twenty-three of this book. This is the first testimony of the finished Bible.

Next in verse seventeen it is written, *"And when he had opened the book."* This is showing you that Jesus is the one to "divide" the Bible and we are the ones to follow His divide. This was covered in depth in chapter twenty-four of this book. We will see that these to whom He was reading would not receive His dividing and follow Him but would rather seek to kill Him. This is the second testimony of the finished Bible.

In verse eighteen and nineteen it is written, *"The Spirit of the Lord is upon me, because he hath anointed me to preach..."* As was covered in depth in chapter twenty-five of this book, Jesus was here dividing to a specific chapter in Isaiah which was sixty-one, in order to match book number sixty-one of the finished Bible, where it says, *"holy men of God spake as they were moved by the Holy Ghost (2 Pet. 1:21)."* Note the content match:

Isaiah chapter 61: The Spirit of the Lord is upon me to preach (Isa. 61:1)

Book number 61: The Holy Ghost moved men of God to speak (2 Pet. 1:21)

Jesus was standing on a double testimony that had not yet manifested in their sight but was present with them in the seed of this chapter of Isaiah that He held in His hands. Jesus was declaring both His authority and was beginning to bring in the authority of the KJV here which He will solidify, as we will see. This is the third testimony of the finished Bible and the first emergence of the KJV.

In verse twenty it is written, *"And he closed the book."* When Jesus closes something as finished, no man can open it, *"he that... shutteth and no man openeth (Rev. 3:7)."* This is a fourth testimony of the finished Bible.

In verse twenty-one it is written, *"This day is this scripture fulfilled in your ears."* The total word count that Jesus spoke in this Luke four passage as the opener, divider, and closer of the finished Bible is a grand total of "sixty-six words" in the King James Bible. Again, we see one word spoken for each of the "sixty-six books" of the finished King James Bible. With these words, Jesus was declaring the authority and fulfillment of the words of Isaiah in Himself and the King James Bible. This is the fifth testimony of the finished Bible, and by note, the second of the King James Bible.

We said back in chapter fourteen, "God had predestinated and called King James." Jesus knew King James before he was born because *"he knew all men (John 2:24)."* When Jesus looked at a man in the days of His flesh, He knew who they were from the eternal. When Jesus looked at a man, He knew whether they were in glory or in the lake of fire. Likewise, Jesus knew the King James Bible in glory as the finished word of God before its time because it is timeless. For Jesus in Luke four to speak the exact words necessary for the maturity of translation to manifest in "sixty-six words," according to the "sixty-six books," to give authority to the King James Version, was as natural for Him as simply speaking according to the Bible.

Do you believe all that you have just read? When Jesus brought forth this great revelation he followed it by sorely chastening the people for their unbelief (Luke 4:23-27). And then they sought to murder Him, *"And all they in the synagogue, when they heard these things, were filled with wrath, And rose up, and thrust him out of the city, and led him unto the brow of the hill whereon their city was built, that they might cast him down headlong (vs. 28,29)."*

Satan was behind those who sought to murder Jesus when he exploited Himself as the honored Messiah figure of the prophet Isaiah and confirmed the authority of the finished Bible in the King James Version. Satan hates Jesus, the Word of God, and he hates the King James Bible, the word of God, and is out to destroy (1 Cor. 10:10). Satan does not hate the other translations of the Bible. He is behind them and using them to take aim at destroying the true Bible and the church, even as he used the first published false Bible in Genesis chapter three to destroy Eve. Ask your own conscience: we have more Bible translations than ever in world history, but is this not the weakest generation of Christians the church has ever seen?

To Satan, the other translations of the Bible do not matter as to what they say because they are not the actual word of God. He is smart enough to know that if something is fake it is not real, no matter how much it looks to be on the outside. Are you? However, everything in the matrix is according to the real word of God in the King James Bible. It does not matter that the other Bibles say that he will be thrown in the lake of fire because they have no authority. They have no authority because they do not source from God. And because they do not source from God they did not grow to maturity on the true vine through history as the real word of God has. What does matter to the Devil is that the King James Bible says he will be thrown in the lake of fire, because this word controls the matrix, and the eternal outcome of everything that is happening in time is according to this Bible. And in the King James Bible, Satan is coded to die and suffer *"everlasting fire, prepared for the devil and his angels (Matt. 25:41)."* This is why we see how even as Satan sought to break Jesus, the Word of God, in the wilderness temptation (Matt. 4/Luke 4), so he is seeking to break the scripture of the King James Bible. But Jesus was not able to be broken by Satan and so likewise, *"the scripture cannot be broken (John 10:35)."*

To die is to suffer the ultimate of defeat. If not rescued by the life of Jesus, to die is to enter everlasting punishment and torment (Matt. 25:46). In death, Jesus will intensify the suffering of Satan and every man who will be held accountable for their sin which caused His own death at the cross, by standing at the shore of the lake of fire justified as *"both Lord and Christ (Acts 2:36)"* to personally witness their agony under the wrath of God (Rev. 14:10). This is what is at stake and this is what it means "to die."

It is common Bible knowledge that the number "5" represents death in the Bible. In Genesis chapter "5" in verse "5" is where the roll out of death begins, *"And all the days that Adam lived were nine hundred and thirty years and he died (Gen. 5:5),"* followed by, *"Seth… and he died (5:8)"* and *"Enos… and he died (5:11)"* and *"Cainan… and he died (5:14)"* and *"Mahalaleel… and he died (5:17)"* and *"Jared… and he died (5:20)"* and *"Methuselah… and he died (5:27)"* and *"Lamech… and he died (5:31)."*

Satan is very aware of this coding and that his name is also coded with a double portion of death. The word "Satan" appears exactly 55 times in the king James Bible. He must break the scripture. Even his name into English in the King James Bible is a binding death certification. With the simple English gematria of "A=1, B=2, C=3, D=4, etc." the value of the word "Satan" also equals "55," showing you again that English is God's destination language for the Bible. By way of guilty association, Judas also equals the value of "55" in English gematria. The word "devils" also appears exactly 55 times in the King James Bible. They are also coded to die the death therefore they must help Satan to break the scripture. Will you help Satan also? Or will you stand firm by faith on the finished Bible, the King James Bible? All who help Satan through their unbelief are tied to him. This means they are led by him. And this means they are following him. When he goes into the lake of fire they will be pulled in with him.

Satan, who is the devil, is a god, but the God of gods has written that he will die like a man, *"I have said, ye are gods... But ye shall die like men... (Ps. 82:6,7)."* Man's death is in his genes; in his 46 chromosomes. The words "the devil" are written 46 times in the King James Bible. On the 46'th usage of the words "the devil," Satan is thrown into the lake of fire, which is the second "death" (Rev. 20:10,14). Not only will he die like men according to the number 46, according to the human chromosomal count which carries the gene of death, but this specific judgment count is retribution for the 46 words that he used to deceive Eve in the garden. We covered this in detail in chapter seventeen of this book. Everywhere Satan turns in the King James Bible he is coded to die the death. Although in our day he has succeeded well at snuffing out the King James Bible from the spirit of the church by drowning it in counterfeits, by grace God will always keep a remnant who will stand in the gap and uphold the true word of God by faith. His time to break the scripture is running out.

Man is also coded to die the death as we read in Genesis 5:5ff, but he is not as vividly aware of this as is Satan; neither is he as smart as Satan:

> *For man also knoweth not his time: as the fishes that are taken in an evil net, and as the birds that are caught in the snare; so are the sons of men snared in an evil time, when it falleth suddenly upon them (Ecc. 9:12)*

Even if a man lives long his day will come, and God is tracking every one of them. We read in Genesis 5:27 that Methuselah died, and he lived longer than any man who saw death, living to be 969 years old. His name is mentioned several times in the first of the Old Testament. Then his name appears one last time in the New Testament, in Luke 3:37, where the death role call from Genesis chapter five is being recited. His name appears as the 969'th word of the chapter in the King James Bible, according to his age at death, 969 years old:

> *Which was the son of Mathusala, which was the son of Enoch, which was the son of Jared, which was the son of Maleleel, which was the son of Cainan (Luke 3:37)*

Notice that the spelling of his name is changed from Methuselah to Mathusala just this one time in the King James Bible to point you to the word "Math." The Spirit encourages you to count to arrive at the conclusion that 969 year old Methuselah is the 969'th word in the chapter, reminding you that God is counting. If God is tracking the days of the oldest man who ever lived and died, he is counting your days too.

But man was not created with the end purpose "to die." God purposed the opposite, "to multiply." In Genesis 1:28 we read, *"And God blessed them, and God said unto them, Be fruitful and multiply."* The word *"multiply"* in the same simple English gematria we covered before equals the value of 128. God again is demonstrating the destination language of the Bible by matching this word that carries the value of 128 in verse 1:28 which He does everywhere in the finished King James Bible. The God who wrote the bible also wrote English. In fact, God used the word *"multiply (Gen. 1:28)"* a total of 46 times in the King James Bible because it relates to chromosomal generation (46 human chromosomes).

As the Master of English and the God who redeems we see that there is a reversal of fortune in the number of death. It is common Bible knowledge that the number "5" also represents grace. It is very common for a single number to have two opposite representations in scripture, a righteous and an evil designation.

In the demonstration of "5" as the number of grace, the Lord grand stands His mastery of the words of the English language. The first usage of the word grace is in Genesis 6:8, *"But Noah found grace in the eyes of the Lord."* Noah is the first man to be associated with grace and it occurs the "5'th" time his name is mentioned. This exclamation is reinforced by Jesus in the

New Testament. Although "Noah" appears in the word of God over fifty times, Jesus changes his name to "Noe" for 5 times in the King James Bible to give a combined Old Testament/New Testament witness. Even in the reference numbers of Genesis 6:8, the first mention of grace and the fifth mention of Noah, we see the number 6 (the number of man) facing the number 8 (the number of Jesus). This in itself is the definition of grace, for a condemned man to meet the savior. By Jesus referring to Noah as Noe for 5 times, He was living out the meaning even down to the numbers of the finished Bible. This is true mastery of the English language.

But not all men are interested in facing Jesus in order to be saved by grace as was Noah but would rather die the devil's death. We mentioned that Satan and Judas both have the same simple English gematria value of 55. Judas has been assigned the same double portion of death as Satan because he is the son of perdition. Jesus prayed this to the Father on the night of His death:

While I was with them in the world, I kept them in thy name: those that thou gavest me I have kept, and none of them is lost, but the son of perdition; that the scripture might be fulfilled (John 17:12)

Just hours before this prayer, Jesus was in the upper room with His disciples for the last supper. Jesus announced His betrayal at hand. The disciple whom Jesus loved then asked Him, *"Lord, who is it? (John 13:25)"*

Jesus answered, He it is to whom I shall give a sop, when I have dipped it. And when he had dipped the sop, he gave it to Judas Iscariot, the son of Simon. And after the sop Satan entered into him… (John 13:26,27)

Jesus was always speaking according to the King James Bible. In the King James Bible, the exact word *"sop"* is used only three times and that to testify that Judas is the *"son of perdition (John 17:12)."* Jesus gave the "S O P" to the "S. O. P." displaying His mastery of the English language before it ever even was in time.

You must choose if "words" is the limit that God payed attention to the Bible unto completion. If you believe all the above is random and accidental, you have departed from faith that God wrote the Bible at this point. Are you really comfortable in your conscience to that decision for all eternity?

Be reminded, all of these examples are but a few of the immeasurable examples of the word of God, in the King James Bible. The scope of this book is not to cover but to convict, that you would simply believe on the true word of God, the King James Bible, before it is too late: *"For whosoever shall be ashamed of me and of my words, of him shall the son of man be ashamed, when he shall come in his own glory, and in his Father's glory, and of the holy angels (Luke 9:26)."* By the way, *"son of man (Luke 9:26)"* in the New Testament of the King James Bible… is written 88 times (the number of Jesus).

CHAPTER 27

LETTERS

> THEN SAID THEY UNTO HIM, SAY NOW SHIBBOLETH; AND HE SAID SIBBOLETH: FOR HE COULD NOT FRAME TO PRONOUNCE IT RIGHT. THEN THEY TOOK HIM, AND SLEW HIM AT THE PASSAGES OF JORDAN: AND THERE FELL AT THAT TIME OF THE EPHRAIMITES FORTY AND TWO THOUSAND
>
> JUDGES 12:6

Proverbs 18:21 says that *"death and life are in the power of the tongue."* In Judges 12, Jephthah the mighty man of valor led his people to put down his brothers of the people Ephraim. After the initial fight, Jephthah's men cut off the necessary passages for the escaped Ephraimites to return to their land. When they would attempt to go through they were border checked to confirm what people they were truly of by being put to the test, *"Say now Shibboleth (Judges 12:6)."* The people of Ephraim could not pronounce one single letter and the word would come out *"Sibboleth."* So, the Proverb was true that *"death and life are in the power of the tongue (Prov. 18:21)."* Yes, because of one single letter, forty-two thousand men were put to death (Judges 12:6).

Similarly, we will all experience that *"death and life are in the power of the tongue."* We can confess the truth with the tongue now and be saved, *"Jesus is Lord (Rom. 10:9)"* or we can confess the truth after we are judged and have perished, *"Jesus is Lord (Phil. 2:11)."* It is also the truth that should be confessed, that the King James Bible is the word of God. However, the professing church is no longer seeking the truth, neither do they love the truth, but are following men. For this cause, God is sending them strong delusion (2 Thess. 2:10,11).

When God sent strong delusion upon Israel, He took away their vision of mind of Him, their clarity in walk with Him, their common sense in relationship with Him:

For the Lord hath poured out upon you the spirit of deep sleep, and hath closed your eyes: the prophets and your rulers, the seers hath he covered. And the vision of all is become unto you as the words of a book that is sealed, which men deliver to one that is learned, saying, Read this, I pray thee: and he saith, I cannot; for it is sealed: And the book is delivered to him that is not learned, saying, Read this, I pray thee: and he saith, I am not learned. Wherefore the Lord said, Forasmuch as this people draw near me with their mouth, and with their lips do honour me, but have removed their heart far from me, and their fear toward me is taught by the precept of men (Isa. 29:10-13)

The more things change, the more they stay the same. Today the *"prophets, rulers, seers, learned, not learned"* of the church *"hath he covered"* from the truth, and the King James Bible, the very word of God, has been concealed from Christians for the glory of God. Every generation has unique trials specific to their age regarding the truth that require those who fall and those who overcome, that God be glorified. We will cover this closely in an upcoming chapter titled "Prophecy."

To believe that God has finished a Holy Bible is to have vision, clarity, and relationship with Him in the midst of a day of delusion. We have seen that the books, book order, chapters, verses and words of the King James Bible are all divinely cut like facets of a jewel and set in exact place. When we hold this truth by faith with our whole heart we become like the prongs of a ring that hold this entire jewel of glory. This then includes us for that great day when the Lord makes up His jewels (Malachi 3:17).

The books, book order, chapters, verses and words of the King James Bible can only matter thanks to letters because letters are the building blocks of them all. In Judges 12:6 death and life were settled over a single letter between man and man. In Galatians 3:16 we see that death and life are settled again over a single letter, this time between man and God.

Now to Abraham and his seed were the promises made. He saith not, And to seeds, as of many; but as of one, And to thy seed, which is Christ (Gal. 3:16)

The Apostle Paul makes distinction by letter to detour from *"seeds, as of many"* which will take you to death, and into *"seed"* singular *"which is Christ"* which will take you to life.

The one letter that makes the difference between death and life in this word, in this verse, in this chapter, in this ordered book of the books, is the letter "s". God is being specific that the letter "s" is not to be added.

The adding of the letter "s" proves to be a point of umbrage with God from the beginning. Genesis 1:1 in the King James Bible says this, *"In the beginning God created the heaven and the earth."* Every other Bible adds the letter "s" and says this, "in the beginning God created the heaven's' and the earth." This artificially added letter "s" of all other Bibles destroys the perfect "letter, vowel, consonant" count match that the first verse of the Bible has with the last verse of the Bible in the King James Bible alone. This throws the Bible off of its feet (we covered the Bible's feet in chapter nineteen of this book).

God will not allow you to even get past Genesis 1:1, the very first verse of the Bible, without letting you know right from the start that He has a controversy with every other Bible on the deepest level of "letters." If we were to go deeper yet, to a level that God sees, the simple English gematria for all the letters of the entire verse of Genesis 1:1 is equal to the 44 letters that make up the verse, which is the value of 411, which can be viewed as 4 x 11 = 44, the grand total returning you to the initial parts, making a cellular circuit. These other Bibles which have added the letter "s" do not pass the geometric test of God and will not make up the jewels of the Lord on that day.

This last example of the depth of letter structure, even rooting themselves in harmony with the destination language of English in His perfected King James Bible, may seem unnecessary to us. However, the word of God is metabolic because it is living, as was covered in chapter seven of this book. In short, this means that there is an internal structuring process which is producing the final words to make a specific quality of energy available to the one who consumes it by his spirit.

This metabolic process and organic functioning and operating of "the word of God" is of an anabolic nature. In short, this means that the structuring process is taking many simple forms and gathering them into a more complex chain, yet a more concentrated form, at the same time. What this means in terms of "the word of God King James Bible" is that specific letters, which make up spellings, which make up words, which make up verses, which make up chapters, which make up books, are of a highly specific and organized and compounded nature so as to work together on a chemical level according to the creator's engineering. When ingested into the spirit of the believer, "the word of God" from God's very own mouth, is entering in to make a spiritual transformation according to its anabolic compound for the release of life. The phrase "the word of God" appears exactly 46 times (the number of man's chromosomes) in the King James Bible because man must have it to live (Matt. 4:4 and cover of this book).

In fact, the anabolic nature of God's word is hyper-anabolic. Building off of the example from our last chapter that the number 5 has the meaning of both death and grace, we can take a passage and reverse engineer it to see how deep the complex construction goes in the King James Bible. Prepare your mind to follow with intensity:

Reverse engineer step 1:

The Bible opens with the first seven verses containing exactly 555 letters in the King James Bible which means death amplified. This is the first three occurrences of the number 5.

Reverse engineer step 2:

Why are there 555 letters in the first seven verses of the King James Bible? Because seven has sEVEn in the middle who brought in death.

Reverse engineer step 3:

sEVEn (se"v"en) has a Latin numeral V (which means 5) in the middle of her name. This is the fourth occurrence of the number 5.

Reverse engineer step 4:

sEVEn has a Roman numeral V with the letter E on both sides of it EVE. E is the fifth letter of the English alphabet making the word seven into s555n. This adds two more occurrences, making six occurrences of the number 5.

Reverse engineer step 5:

EVE (555) partook of death when she partook of the tree of the knowledge of good and evil. The lower-case usage of the words "good" and "evil" as it is written in God's forbidding command (Gen. 2:17) is found in exactly 555 chapters of the King James Bible. This adds three more occurrences, making nine occurrences of the number 5.

Reverse engineer step 6:

The King James Bible has exactly 31102 chapters. If you divide the total number of chapters of the King James Bible there are exactly 15551 chapters on Eve's side, the left side, representing the Old Testament and death, and there are exactly 15551 chapters on Christ's side, the right side, representing the New Testament and grace. This adds six more occurrences, making fifteen occurrences of the number 5.

Reverse engineer step 7:

The Bible closes with the last 5 verses of the Bible containing exactly 555 letters in the King James Bible which means grace. This adds four more occurrences, making nineteen occurrences of the number 5.

Reverse engineer step 8:

Why are there 555 letters in the last 5 verses? Because Christ is God's grace (who came in the fifth millennium). The word Christ appears exactly 555 times in the King James Bible. This adds three more occurrences, making twenty-two occurrences of the number 5.

We have just reverse engineered a twenty-two hyper anabolic compound of Genesis 1:1-7 in the KJV. We have seen in this exactness of letters the precision and inclusion of: Latin which points us back to Pilate's sign which was nailed to the cross; English which was the destination language as indicated by the Latin on Pilate's sign which was nailed to the cross; doctrinal harmony in the lay out of the finished Bible from death to grace; over all verse balance in relationship to the beginning and ending of the finished Bible; and more. There is absolutely no room for a free radical letter "s" to be in Genesis 1:1.

Do you believe God took His hands and eyes and mind and heart away from the total control of finishing the Bible at this point? Is this too, merely circumstantial coincidence? Evil unbelief can never be cured by evidence and true faith from the Father needs but little to grow big and strong. Which one are you now that God is narrowing us into even the scrutiny of letters?

As each chapter has closed reminding you, these examples which are baffling to us are only shallow examples to God of the never-ending examples of the word of God, in the King James Bible. The scope of this book is to show enough for you to ask the Spirit for a crucified mind that you may put off the false Bible's and for the resurrection mind of Christ that you may put on the true word of God. You do not need to know all of these anabolic ingredients of the King James Bible in order for them to work in you, but you must believe.

CHAPTER 28

NUMBERS

BUT THE VERY HAIRS OF YOUR HEAD
ARE ALL NUMBERED

MATTHEW 10:30

There is a great divide in the mind of most Christians. This divide is that the letters of the Bible are very important because they make up words which reveal the truth but numbers in scripture are not important but even taboo. Let this same Christian try and live a single day of his life ignoring numbers with their meanings and his life will be a disaster. An average American uses and depends on numbers countless times a day and it is no stretch to say that all of life depends on them.

On the lighter side, culturally speaking, numbers carry meaning as much as words do. In most states of the USA: if I say 16 this means "age of driving"; if I say 18 this means "age of adult"; if I say 21 this means "age of drinking"; if I say 40 this means "age of over the hill"; if I say 65 this means "age of retirement."

God is no less the author of numbers than He is of letters. As the author, He is the one to ascribe their meaning. When we come to God's word to know and understand their meanings according to His discerning, we are righteous. This is called "number-ology" which means "words about numbers." If we turn deviant with numbers or superstitious with numbers, this is called "numerology," and this is evil. Just as we saw in the last chapter, oh what a difference a single letter can make.

Numbers are the wisdom of God. He has even named an entire book of the Bible after them, the book of "Numbers." In God's acts, words and numbers must work together in order that the meaning of the one reinforces the meaning of the other and reverse wise. For example, when God says this in words, *"an innumerable company of angels (Heb. 12:22),"* the words He speaks must be congruent with the numbers, *"And his tail drew the third part of the stars of heaven, and did cast them to the earth (Rev. 12:4)."* In this example, the word *"innumerable"* speaking of the angels, and the number "the third" numbering the fallen angels, are congruent because 1/3 is an innumerable number being 33.3333333 into infinity.

Jesus was wrapped in numbers. We saw in chapter twenty-three of this book all of the "threes" He came to fulfill according to the Levitical priesthood and the offerings, according to the scriptures. Once again, in this we see how numbers and words have relationship to each other and reinforcement of meaning. "Three" is a number, and Jesus is the "Word." This is "number" and "word" bonding. All of the "threes" that Jesus was wrapped in were man's spiritual imperfections and the evil meaning of "three." When He rose again on the "third" day, He was now wrapped in the righteous meaning of the same number "three," as in the word "Godhead," which is written exactly "three" times in the King James Bible (Acts 17:29; Rom. 1:20; Col. 2:9). And as in the words "Ancient of days" which is written exactly "three" times in the King James Bible (Dan. 7:9,13,22). And as the "thrice" usage of the words, "Holy, holy, holy" in the same verse is exactly "three" times in the King James Bible (Isa. 6:3; Ez. 39:7; Rev. 4:8). And as the word "Christian(s)" which is written exactly "three" times in the King James Bible (Acts 11:26; 26:28; 1 Pet. 4:16). And as the words "born again" which is written exactly "three" times in the King James Bible (John 3:3,7; 1 Pet. 1:23). And as the words "resurrection from the dead" which is written exactly "three" times in the King James Bible (Luke 20:35; Acts 4:2; Rom. 1:4). All of these are objects of spiritual perfection and the opposite of evil. We said two chapters ago that a single number may have two opposite representations in scripture, a righteous and an evil designation, and here we see it again. What is important for us to see here is that there is a divine relationship between the numbers and the words and nothing is random or arbitrary.

Even the Father has wrapped Himself in numbers in the Bible, even an infinity of numbers. The God who defines Himself as the undefinable *"I AM THAT I AM"* has done so to the uncapturable sum of π (PI). Because π has an infinite number of digits in its decimal representation, and π does not settle into a repeating pattern, but irrationally continues without end, it is a mathematical marvel and the only worthy number representation for the Father, who is *"I AM THAT I AM."* When abbreviated for common reference sake π = 3.14 or 3.1415 as in Exodus 3:14,15 which is the revelation of all revelations:

And God said unto Moses, I AM THAT I AM: and he said, Thus shalt thou say unto the children of Israel, I AM hath sent me unto you. And God said moreover unto Moses, Thus shalt thou say unto the children of Israel, The LORD God of your fathers, the God of Abraham, the God of Isaac, and the God of Jacob, hath sent me unto you: this is my name for ever, and this is my memorial unto all generations. (Ex. 3:14,15 π =3.1415)

Plain words have their meanings magnified and deepened and expanded by numbers and even bring out the thoughts and intentions of the heart. If someone is pushed once it is an accident; pushed twice it is a coincidence; pushed three times and someone has some explaining to do; pushed four times and words are getting exchanged; pushed five times and there is a fight. The number of occurrences is a form of communication that magnifies, deepens and expands the meaning of what is being said as well as divulges the motives in any given situation or text. Here is an example of a fight that started from five pushes, five "I will" statements, when Lucifer fell from heaven:

For thou hast said in thine heart, I will ascend into heaven, I will exalt my throne above the stars of God: I will sit also upon the mount of the congregation, in the sides of the North: I will ascend above the heights of the clouds; I will be like the most high (Isa. 14:13,14)

Knowing that Lucifer boasted five times (the number of death) with five "I" statements, read the following passage of the Pharisee who is pushing his own self-righteousness on God:

The Pharisee stood and prayed thus with himself, God, I thank thee, that I am not as other men are, extortioners, unjust, adulterers, or even as this publican. I fast twice in the week, I give tithes of all that I possess (Luke 18:11,12)

The Pharisee uses the personal pronoun "I" five times. Lucifer has five "I" statements and the Pharisee has five "I" statements. By linking the common denominator between Lucifer and the Pharisee by the joining of words and numbers, we see that the Pharisee is not only self-righteous in plain words, but by number count he has the being and motives of Satan and is one in death with Satan and is the expression of Satan. The number five extracts the thoughts and intentions of the heart of the Pharisee in this passage and numbers him for death with the original transgressor (Isa. 53:12).

In this book, there has been many foregone conclusions and confirmations as a result of counting which have enhanced meaning, and guided wisdom into the King James Bible as the very word of God. We have sampled the counting of books of the Bible, chapters of the Bible, words of the Bible, letters of the Bible. We have even sampled counting the simple gematria of the destination language of English in the Bible. All of these have contributed together toward knowledge in the matter of the finished King James Bible.

English, as the destination language for the matured Bible, is a divine language. God wrote the English language. Specifically, with the simple English gematria, this of course means that God has also numbered every single letter of the English language. This is by no means a first for God.

God wrote the Hebrew language also, the seed of the Bible, the Old Testament. When He did this, unlike English, He left it without numeric symbols, but not without numeric values. God numbered every single letter of the Hebrew language building the value of numbers into the letters. Therefore, gematria was employed by God in the seed. Here is an example of a Hebrew Old Testament scripture that has no numbers in it, only letters doubling as numbers:

Now the weight of gold that came to Solomon in one year was six hundred threescore and six talents of gold (1 Kings 10:14)

The weight of the gold was 666 talents, but no numbers appear in this verse, only letters carrying numeric value.

God wrote the Greek language yet also, the growth of the Bible, the New Testament, and He did the same thing again here. He left this language also without numeric symbols and like Hebrew, ascribed a numeric value to each letter of the alphabet. Gematria was employed by God also in the growth. Here is an example of a Greek New Testament scripture, even the "mate" of 1 Kings 10:14, that has no numbers in it, only letters doubling as numbers:

Here is wisdom, Let him that hath understanding count the number of the beast: for it is the number of a man; and his number is Six hundred threescore and six (Rev. 13:18)

The number of the beast is 666, but no numbers appear in this verse, only alpha numeric value. In both cases, the Hebrew seed and the Greek growth, the numbers are present in the words. So reverse wise, many words are being spoken in the numbers, such as the numbers 1611 (as in the 1611 King James Holy Bible), which we will see in the next chapter.

God has reverenced gematria with these two scriptures that mate for a testimony. It has been noted several times in this book that "Jesus" is represented by the number "8." As much as is possible, we are building revelation on top of revelation for the sake of spiritual illumination and understanding. In the New Testament Greek, the word "Jesus" carries the alpha numeric value of "888." Therefore, we should not be surprised at all that the words "In His Name" appears in exactly "8" verses in "8" chapters in "8" books of the exalted King James Bible. This number "888" is strengthening and over flowing power into these words: *"I am come in my Father's name, and ye receive me not: if another shall come in his own name, him ye will receive (John 5:43)."*

Jesus is the anointed one who has come "In His Name" and the King James Bible is the anointed Bible that has come "In His Name." In both cases, we must not receive another (John 5:43). The King James Bible has inherited its interaction and role playing of words and numbers in relationship, even gematria life, from the genes of the seed and the growth of the line of the Bible.

A final closing reminder. The examples we have covered in books, chapters, verses, words, letters, and now numbers, are a minor amount of the overwhelmingly complex nature of the finished Bible, the King James Bible. Each of the past chapters are not a finished subject but are for laying a foundation for you to build upon. They are also for making clear and plain to any honest heart that at no time in any of the process of the Bible throughout history, has God ever taken his absolute God controlling hand off of His word which matured in the KJV, nor made a man the lead of His word ever. When you deny the King James Bible its exclusive authority as the word of God of Him and give your heart and soul and mind and strength to another Bible, you are playing the harlot with a God who has said, *"…the Lord, whose name is Jealous, is a jealous God (Ex. 34:14)."*

CHAPTER 29

THE YEAR 1611

BUT GOD HATH CHOSEN THE FOOLISH
THINGS OF THE WORLD TO CONFOUND
THE WISE; AND GOD HATH CHOSEN
THE WEAK THINGS OF THE WORLD
TO CONFOUND THE THINGS WHICH
ARE MIGHTY; AND BASE THINGS OF
THE WORLD, AND THINGS WHICH ARE
DESPISED, HATH GOD CHOSEN, YEA, AND
THINGS WHICH ARE NOT, TO BRING TO
NOUGHT THINGS THAT ARE: THAT NO
FLESH SHOULD GLORY IN HIS PRESENCE

1 CORINTHIANS 1:27-29

Process this question with all fear and trepidation: Has God called you to translate the Bible?

When you espouse that the King James Bible has inherent errors and you change translation (add) or deny accuracy of certain verses, words, spellings, numbers (take away), this is exactly what you are demonstrating you believe in your heart, that God has called you to translate the Bible.

The error of your way is that you do not know God well: *"interpretations belong to God (Gen. 40:8)."* Spiritual blindness, spiritual ignorance, or worse, spiritual pride, are keeping you from walking in step with God. He has not called you to translate the Bible, this is out of step with where we are in time. He has called you to believe on the Bible He has translated, that you may walk in step with Him in your day.

However, there was a day when men were called to translate the Bible. That monumental day was over four hundred years ago, in the year 1611. Yes, these men were called by God to translate under the inspiration of the Holy Ghost. Do you dare to claim this each time you suggest a better translation?

Even the men themselves who wrote the King James Bible did not dare to claim that they were called by God to write inspired scripture, but they were. Did Matthew or Mark or Luke or John ever claim anywhere in the Bible that God called them to write inspired scripture? But they were too. Often times, it is not until after the fact that we come to understand that God Himself was indeed in the midst thereof. For examples of this, see: Gen. 50:20; Ex. 7:5; Judges 14:2-4; Dan. 3:17-25; Matt. 27:54; Luke 24:15,16-31; etc.

The fact that God inspires translations is obvious within the pages of the scriptures. *"Emmanuel, which being interpreted is, God with us (Matt. 1:23). Talitha cumi; which is, being interpreted, Damsel, I say to thee, arise (Mark 5:41). Golgotha, which is, being interpreted, the place of a skull (Mark 15:22). Eloi, Eloi, lama sabachtani? Which is, being interpreted, My God my God, why hast thou forsaken me? (Mark 15:34). Rabbi, (which is to say, being interpreted, Master,) (John 1:38). Messias, which is, being interpreted, the Christ (John 1:41). Cephas, which is by interpretation, A stone (John 1:42). Siloam, (which is by interpretation, Sent.) (John 9:7). Barnabas, (which is, being interpreted, The son of consolation,) (Acts 4:36). Tabitha, which by interpretation is called Dorcas (Acts 9:36). Elymas the sorcerer (for so is his name by interpretation) (Acts 13:8)."* Etc., etc. In Genesis 42:23 Joseph spoke Egyptian and the Spirit interpreted it into Hebrew recorded scripture. In Daniel 5:26 Aramaic is interpreted by the Spirit into

Hebrew recorded scripture. In Acts, both Paul and Jesus spoke Hebrew and the Spirit interpreted it into Greek recorded scripture (21:40; 26:14). Additionally, scores of Old Testament Hebrew prophecies are recited into New Testament Greek, even loosely recited which in most cases introduces words not in the original (sample Micah 5:2 and Matt. 2:6). With just these limited examples we see that God uses the word *"interpret"* the way we use the word "translate," and that God inspires, double inspires, and even multi inspires interpretations (translations). He is sovereign to do this because *"interpretations belong to God (Gen. 40:8)."* As all of the above demonstrates, it would be crucial that in 1 Corinthians 12:10, the Spirit of God would give the church the gift of *"the interpretation of tongues."* The fruit of this gift would culminate in the one of a kind work of God in the King James Bible as God's translation and divine.

If you know God well, you are aware that He makes very profound one of a kind moves like this. Further example wise, in the move of God, humans alone qualify to be the honored recipients of inheriting God's divine nature through His Son, conforming them to His image in resurrection life and glory (2 Pet. 1:4; Rom. 8:29,30). All other creatures, including the angelic divisions, must look up to the exclusive preeminence of this creature, the sons of God, as only this creature is the perfect expression of Jesus, the Word of God.

In the same way, God sanctified the English language to be the honorific language that all other languages were to look up to, as His calling and election for the perfect expression of the Bible, the word of God. Whether cognoscente of this or not, the world has inherited its own lead according to and as a result of God's decision of English for the Bible. The sun would never set on the British empire through their Imperialist rule. Democracy would spread to be the stabilization of the table of nations. All time zones would become based on Greenwich England time (GMT) as well as the prime meridian of the world. Western superiority and favor and prosperity and charity would succeed for centuries. And in our day, English would become the "lingua franca" of humanity, which means "the common language that the world meets on to communicate with each other." All of this is the direct result of the manifesting of the perfect word of God in the 1611 King James Bible.

I cannot emphasize this enough: do not think that God chose English for the finished Bible for pragmatic reasons, knowing that more people in the world would speak English together than any other language. The influence of the West and the phenomena of "lingua franca" is a direct reflection of God's sovereign move of the English finished Bible and is the overflow of this blessing to the world, and not the other way around.

God always sets the standard. Similar to the wave the world still experiences today from God finishing the Bible in English, we see that when Jesus Christ, the Word of God manifested, the world conformed to the usage of B.C. and A.D. around Him. The first means "Before Christ" and the latter means "Anno Domini – In The Year Of The Lord."

This takes us to the cover of this book and the year 1611 A.D. This year would forever brand mark the famous name of the King James Bible, "The 1611 Authorized Version." There is a term in Galatians 4:4 that says, *"But when the fullness of the time was come."* This is referring to God's perfect timing for sending forth His Son, the Word of God. He did not come too soon, and He did not come too late. God has His timing for all things.

Certainly, this divine timing factor applies to the Bible as well. There is one flagship verse repeated three times in the word of God, which make up the declaration and testimony of the inspiration and inerrancy of the Bible, *"in the mouth of two or three witnesses (Matt. 18:16; 2 Cor. 13:1)."* This one voice spoken three times is as follows:

And Jesus answered him, saying, It is written, That man shall not live by bread alone, but by every word of God (Luke 4:4)

But he answered and said, It is written, Man shall not live by bread alone, but by every word that proceedeth out of the mouth of God (Matt. 4:4)

And he humbled thee, and suffered thee to hunger, and fed thee with manna, which thou knewest not, neither did thy fathers know; that he might make thee know that man doth not live by bread only, but by every word that proceedeth out of the mouth of the Lord doth man live (Deut. 8:3)

When the references of these three flag ship verses are added from top to bottom they equal the year 1611 and are a stamp and a seal of authority that are to be respected and feared:

Luke 4:4
Matt. 4:4
<u>Deut. 8:3</u>
    16:11 or 1611

For the Spirit of God to manifest this sign, wonder, miracle, Moses need be led to write this part of the Torah exactly where he did. Matthew need be led to write this part of his gospel exactly where he did. Luke need be led to write this part of his gospel exactly where he did. None of them had premonition of what the Spirit of God was doing.

To add infinite complexity to this intricacy, when the references of these three flag ship verses are added from left to right, they again equal the year 1611 for a double indemnity of badging of authority for your own warning sake:

Luke 4:4 = 8
Matt. 4:4 = 8   8+8 = 16
Deut. 8:3 = 11   11 = 11   or...   1611

These are the official three flagship verses for the inspiration and inerrancy of the Bible. This achievement required exactness of chapter, verse, and numbering settlement at the very least, not to mention the coalition and divine control of world history and the elapsing of its events, all things Bible. All modern Bible translations number this out because even the Satanic counterfeits must bow the knee and confess which Bible is of the truth.

In addition to these official flagship verses, the Lord God has an official flagship chapter of the Bible to the same testimony. This flagship chapter is

Psalm 119. This is the longest chapter of the entire Bible and is obsessively committed to extolling the absolute greatness and absolute supremacy of God's eternal word. Here are but a few of the Psalm 119 score of famous verses:

Wherewithal shall a young man cleanse his way? By taking heed thereto according to thy word (Psalm 119:9)

Thy word have I hid in mine heart, that I might not sin against thee (Psalm 119:11)

Open thou mine eyes, that I may behold wondrous things out of thy law (Psalm 119:18)

Before I was afflicted I went astray: but now I have kept thy word (Psalm 119:67)

For ever, O Lord, thy word is settled in heaven (Psalm 119:89)

I have more understanding than all my teachers: for thy testimonies are my meditation (Psalm 119:99)

Thy word is a lamp unto my feet, and a light unto my path (Psalm 119:105)

The entrance of thy words giveth light; it giveth understanding unto the simple (Psalm 119:130)

Thy word is very pure: therefore thy servant loveth it (Psalm 119:140)

Thy word is true from the beginning: and every one of thy righteous judgments endureth forever (Psalm 119:160)

Great peace have they which love thy law: and nothing shall offend them (Psalm 119:165)

God has chosen His flagship chapter, Psalm 119, the longest chapter in the Bible, in which nearly every single verse exalts His word, to be grand master divided into exactly 176 verses. These 176 verses should be perceived spiritually in this way:

1611 or 16 x 11 = 176 verses of Psalm 119

The 1611 King James Bible Authorized Version was being testified to all the way back even out of the writer of the 176 verses (16 x 11) of Psalm 119, King David, *"a prophet (Acts 2:30)."* Again, as stated paragraphs ago, even a prophet may not know until long after the fact that God Himself was indeed in the midst thereof. Did the prophet David know He was testifying to the authority of the finished Bible, the 1611 King James Version? No. Was the prophet David testifying to the authority of the finished Bible, the 1611 King James Version? Yes. As mentioned above, every modern day false Bible must confess this and give way to the 1611, whereby confessing the King James Bible as God's word alone. This is the nature of prophecy. The nature of prophecy is tremendously frightening as it involves you unawares. This is to be covered in the next chapter.

This is the point of the book that you literally drop it out of your hands and fall to your knees and repent with tears unto the God of the 1611 King James Bible, *"Rivers of waters run down mine eyes, because they keep not thy law (Psalm 119:136)."* The Bible you hold in your hands is the *"law"* you *"keep."* If it is not the KJV it will be said of you *"they keep not thy law."* I feel very, very sorry for you if you do not this, and your calloused mind and heart continue on in your NIV law, NASB law, ESV law, NKJV law, etc., etc. May God have mercy on your soul.

Ye hypocrites, ye can discern the face of the sky and of the earth; but how is it that ye do not discern this time? (Luke 12:56)

Jesus scowled the people of His day for not recognizing the time of His coming, the Word of God. We can be sure that He will scowl the people today for not recognizing the time of the year 1611 A.D. and the Bible's coming, the word of God.

CHAPTER 30

PROPHECY

And In Them Is Fulfilled The Prophecy Of Esaias, Which Saith, By Hearing Ye Shall Hear, And Shall Not Understand; And Seeing Ye Shall See, And Shall Not Perceive

Matthew 13:14

The last chapter ended with these chilling words, "the nature of prophecy is tremendously frightening."

Not even the law should strike fear in our hearts as much as prophecy. The law is straight forward to man: it is held by man (Rom. 1:18); it is manifest in man (1:19); it is in the nature of man (2:14); it is written in the heart of man (2:15). When you break the law, you choose to do so well aware.

But not so with prophecy. The nature of prophecy is to visit you without you having perception of its presence, and this is tremendously frightening (Luke 19:41-44). The nature of prophecy is to overtake you by stealth, only for you to discover when it is too late, and this is terribly horrifying (Matt. 7:21-23). The nature of prophecy is to favor only the few who have paid strict attention to special revelation whole heartedly, and not to be in this remnant is terrifying (Isa. 6:9-13).

Read the following:

But of the tree of the knowledge of good and evil, thou shalt not eat of it: for in the day that thou eatest thereof thou shalt surely die (Gen. 2:17)

The law is straight forward, *"But of the tree of the knowledge of good and evil, thou shalt not eat of it."* The prophecy is without perception, *"for in the day that thou eatest thereof thou shalt surely die."* The words do not read "if thou eatest" but *"in the day that thou eatest."* These words were a prophecy.

God spoke this prophecy over Adam. At the hearing of these words, Adam should have asked God to save him from His prophecy, but Adam was without perception. Have you ever prayed to be saved from God's prophecies? Are you even aware that you need to be saved from God's prophecies?

Watch ye therefore, and pray always, that ye may be accounted worthy to escape all these things that shall come to pass, and to stand before the son of man (Luke 21:36)

In Luke twenty-one Jesus reveals prophecy after prophecy after prophecy, then concludes with the above warning to ask to be saved from His prophecies, *"pray always."* Toward the very end of His prophecy arrangement, and taking special aim at the last days generation, is this specific prophecy:

Heaven and earth shall pass away: but my words shall not pass away (Luke 21:33)

Without a doubt, this prophecy fits the last days generation where the battle royal is the battle for the Bible. Sadly, this battle is not relegated to the world but further disgraced in the church as the battle royal is discovered to be for nothing less than the King James Bible, the only true Bible, the finished Bible.

Jesus picks up on His prophecy, *"my words shall not pass away (Luke 21:33),"* and reissues it to the last days generation, in the seven letters to the seven churches in the book of Revelation chapters two and three.

In the literal, these seven churches are individual local churches that embodied the content of the specific letter addressed to them, for better or for worse.

In the prophetic, these seven churches picture the one universal church of all time that embodies the content of all the letters, for better or for worse. The consecutive nature of the letters from one to seven displays a chronology chart of the one universal church's earthly ministry from beginning to end.

The prophetic is not to say that a last day's local church cannot suffer from things that affected a first day's local church in the literal sense. The prophetic is to reveal the aggregate condition of the professed body of Christ through history and is vision at large.

In the literal, it is in Jesus' letters to the last two local churches, the church in Philadelphia and the church of the Laodiceans, that Jesus sheds light on His original prophecy, *"my words shall not pass away (Luke 21:33)."* In the literal, seeds were growing for the springing of prophecy. In the prophetic, Jesus' last two letters cover the last span of the one universal church's earthly days, and thus the last days generation. Therefore, this prophecy hangs over our heads.

While the majority of the seven churches received burning chastisement by the Lord Jesus Christ, only the church in Philadelphia reaches the height of accolade from the Master (Not even the church in Smyrna is exalted so highly).

Chronologically laid out over world history, this puts the church in Philadelphia, the second to last church age, at the time that the 1611 King James Bible was written and finished. The literal commendation Jesus gave the church in Philadelphia originally was then prophetically fulfilled in time by the one universal church according to its stage:

For thou... hast kept my word (Rev. 3:8)

This prophetic *"church in Philadelphia"* would be the guardian of the word of God. For millennium after millennium God painstakingly and with much longsuffering took His word from seed, to growth to maturity and they were the keepers:

Thou hast kept the word of my patience (Rev. 3:10)

At last, the perfect word of God had taken its place at the center of worship in the church. From this nucleus position, for centuries to come until our day, the finished Bible would reach the world through the prophetic *"church in Philadelphia."*

The world would see the likes of the multitude, of the glory of Christian battle, by the sword of the Spirit, such as: the life and blood and tears and prayers of William Tyndale which are poured into the pages of the King James Bible; the Puritans, though known for the Geneva Bible, who yet played a key influential role in the translation, publishing and embarking success of the King James Bible; John Bunyan who published Pilgrim's Progress; John Wesley and Charles Wesley and the greatness of the hymns of the faith; George Whitfield and revival; Jonathan Edwards and the Great Awakening; George Frederick Handle who composed the classic concerto "Messiah," a master piece to the text of the King James Bible; A King James Bible literate population that backboned the construction of the United States constitution; Charles Finney and the Second Great Awakening; missionary movement by William Carey, Hudson Taylor, David Livingstone, and countless more, taking the King James Bible to the tongues of the world for massive deployment of the great commission; Charles Spurgeon, D.L. Moody, and landmark men and women of the faith; The Gideons who covered the land with the King James Bible; *"And what shall I more say? for the time would fail me to tell of Gedeon... ... (Heb. 11:32)"* etc., etc.

Sorrowfully, the world would never see the likes of such again. According to prophecy, the last and worst church age would take stage and the one universal *"church in Philadelphia"* would transition into the one universal *"church of the Laodiceans."*

This generation church would be marked by an abhorrent condition: lukewarm; worldly; counterfeit; self-deceived; wretched; miserable; poor; blind; naked. And all of this, ironically, in Jesus' name.

Worst of all, beyond contempt, and beyond the unthinkable, the Word of God would be thrown out of the church in the hour of this prophetic church's watch:

Behold, I stand at the door, and knock (Rev. 3:20)

By now you should well understand that if Jesus, the Word of God is outside the church knocking, the Bible, the word of God is also outside the church knocking. The Bible is the voice of Jesus:

Behold, I stand at the door, and knock: if any man hear my voice… (Rev. 3:20)

It was during this stage of the church, the end of days, that a generation would remove what God had spent thousands of years raising up, the KJV. Counterfeit Bibles would battle ram their way into the church for a century until finally succeeding mainstream in the church from circa 1970 unto our day. This foolish dismount of the finished Bible was the fulfillment of prophecy in a generation, leaving their children with an imitation sword to fight the Devil.

Back to back, from the highest condition to the lowest condition, the *"church in Philadelphia"* kept the word, the *"church of the Laodiceans"* removed the Word. What actually took place?

In the prophetic, with the crowning of the 1611 King James Bible, the finished word of God, the Lord had ordained the English-speaking portion of the body of Christ to be in the most unique place of calling and grace in the body of Christ world-wide and history-wide.

In the office of calling, the English-speaking church was the pastor of the world-wide body of Christ. The very pattern God had imposed on the local level of the churches in the pastoral epistles was in effect in the one universal church as a whole, *"And he gave some… pastors and teachers (Eph. 4:11)."* Along with the finished Bible in the English tongue was committed unto them the shepherding responsibility of feeding God's word to the lambs of the world, *"for the perfecting of the saints, for the work of the ministry, for the edifying of the body of Christ: till we all come in the unity of the faith, and of the knowledge of the Son of God, unto a perfect man, unto the measure of the stature of the fullness of Christ (vs. 12,13)."*

In the gifting of grace, the Western portion of the body of Christ had been equipped to serve above and beyond the other members. All of the following is from 1 Corinthians chapter twelve and the *"diversity of gifts"* of the Spirit. In the *"differences of administrations,"* the English-speaking body of Christ was graced the custodial administration of the perfect word of God, the King James Bible. In the *"diversities of operations"* the English-speaking body of Christ was graced to mobilize this Bible throughout the body of Christ across the face of the earth. *"The manifestation of the Spirit is given to every man to profit withal"* and unto them, the portion of the Spirit's manifesting was the matured Bible and it was their duty to perpetuate it to the next generation of the church. The most unique gracing of *"the word of wisdom"* and *"the word of knowledge"* had been shared with them for the body's sake. *"Prophecy"* and *"the interpretation of tongues"* was given to them grace for grace. The Spirit had blessed this period of the church *"dividing severally as he will"* giving them a critical lead in church history which was to be held against the kingdom of darkness to the end of the age. *"For the body is not one member but many"* and the world needed the Bible that was in the hands of the West. And God was pleased to grant the deliverance of the portion of the body throughout the world through the English-speaking church because *"God set the members every one of them in the body, as it hath pleased him."*

This sense of "office of calling" and "gifting of grace" as the leading portion of the body of Christ waxed and waned and softened over the years into today's cavity condition. And now, all that the lukewarm *"church of the*

Laodiceans" can say regarding the authority and inerrancy of the Bible is, "it doesn't matter which Bible you read (existentialism)" or "they are all good as long as it is good for you (pragmatism)" or "I prefer to interpret the Hebrew or Greek in this way (relativism)." The theories that now mark the age also mark the bibliology of the church.

There will be no revival in the end of the age, in your country, in your state, in your city, in your community, because the English portion of the corporate church repents not of her putting out of the church the very word of God, the King James Bible. This is a terrible sin of the English portion of the corporate church and will affect the world-wide portion of the corporate church. According to the back to back prophecy of the *"church in Philadelphia"* and *"the church of the Laodiceans"* nothing has been learned from Israel's downfall but would only be repeated:

Jesus saith unto them, Did ye never read in the scriptures, the stone which the builders rejected, the same is become the head of the corner: this is the Lord's doing, and it is marvelous in our eyes? (Matt. 21:42)

Corporate Israel rejected Jesus, the Word of God, and the corporate church rejects the King James Bible, the word of God. Do you want to escape this prophecy? The corporate church will not escape this prophecy because it is written not only that the Laodicean church age would be the last church age, but that she would only be fit for removal like the unimaginably disrespectful gentile queen Vashti (a picture of the church's removal), only to be replaced by the Jewish queen Hadassah (a picture of Israel's reinstatement), in Esther 1:19. This is prophecy on top of prophecy against the church. And *"this is the Lord's doing (Matt. 21:42)."* Although the corporate church will not escape, you as an individual can! Jesus' calling out of the sin of the corporate Laodicean church is concluded with an isolated call to individuals to be saved from His prophecy:

Behold, I stand at the door, and knock: if any man hear my voice, and open the door, I will come in to him, and will sup with him, and he with me. To him that overcometh will I grant to sit with me in my throne, even as I also overcame, and am set down with my Father in his throne. He that hath an ear, let him hear what the Spirit saith unto the churches (Rev. 3:20-22)

All of the Lord's calling to repentance is targeted to individuals as shown by the usage of singular terms, *"any man... him... him... he... him... He... him."* All of these are presupposing that the prophecy will sweep away the majority leaving a remnant who paid very close attention in the fear of the Lord. Don't expect your pastor to lead your whole local church out of this prophecy together. You will have to make this move yourself.

We are in an age when men and women are lifting their ministries and ministry names above God's word, cleverly in Jesus' name. They perpetuate a front that they are about the Bible, but they are about themselves. They have big buildings, they have catchy names, they have corporate logo and branding and graphics, they have credentials. With all this they have shown out and lime lighted themselves over the word of God the King James Bible. This is the substance and the spirit of the Laodicean church at work.

You too are still of the Laodicean church if you have a "too big to fail" or "too big to be wrong" corporate mentality regarding the church vs. the King James Bible. Be sure that if unbelief in the matter is what you want in the depth of your heart, God will make room for you to have it. God does not answer every question specifically for this reason. Whatever your reason or justification may be for unbelief in the KJV, you have not understood the nature of prophecy and the role it is playing in this issue. The nature of prophecy is for most to be left out. A careful searching of the scriptures from beginning to end will teach you that the majority case is never ever right no matter how many are in agreement, nor whomever they may be by name. It is always in favor and defense of the one who is out numbered but standing with God who is right. This is prophecy.

Chapter 31

Trial

> And I will bring the third part through the fire, and will refine them as silver is refined, and will try them as gold is tried: they shall call on my name, and I will hear them: I will say, It is my people: and they shall say, The LORD is my God
>
> Zechariah 13:9

Prophecy is a double-edged sword and on the other side of the prophecy blade is trial. Every prophecy is a trial once you have awoken to it.

If you are a soul that has been called to salvation, you learned long ago that the Genesis to Revelation journey of man is a consuming trial from beginning to end. God is exalted above, and every man is in peril below, overseen in a trial of thrones:

> *The LORD is in his holy temple, the LORD'S throne is in heaven: his eyes behold, his eyelids try, the children of men (Psalm 11:4)*

Mankind lives oblivious to the trial of thrones he is in because his "self" deflects his attention to the matter of domestic affairs, such as: family, relationships, sports, entertainment, technology, hobbies, travel, food, education, career, investing, filling the life of the soul and the life of the flesh with all it can get out of this world.

As a member of mankind, this means that the trial of thrones is fixated on you from the beginning of your life to its end, with Christ Jesus and the word of God at its center, for the glory of God. Whether you know it or not (prophecy) or whether you like it or not (trial), God has volunteered you to enter His straight gate (Matt. 7:13), bear His cross (Luke 9:23), go His course (2 Tim. 4:7), run His race (Heb. 12:1), fight His fight (1 Tim. 6:12), wrestle His enemy (Ephes. 6:12), wage His war (1 Pet. 2:11), come into His mystery (Rom. 16:25), receive His revelation (Rev. 1:1), strive according to His word (2 Tim. 2:5), overcome by His Son's life (1 John 5:4), occupy His destiny (Rev. 20:15).

As it pertains to the topic of this book, the trial at hand is the finished word of God, the King James Bible, if you are awake to the prophecy of the last days generation of the Laodicean church hour (Rev. 3:8 vs. Rev. 3:20).

It is true that every generation has temptations *"such as is common to man (1 Cor. 10:13)."* However, it is also true that every generation has temptations and trials unique to their jurisdiction in time. This is the effect of progressive revelation.

Progressive revelation means that from one generation to the next, God has progressively made clearer and clearer His revelation and mystery of the faith (Rom. 16:25,26). This places each passing generation with a maximized amount of responsibility, answerability, charge and duty to God, unrequired by a previous generation:

For unto whomsoever much is given, of him shall be much required - JESUS (Luke 12:48)

An hour is coming when that which is prophecy to this generation will become trial for the next. That generation will experience unparalleled trial like no other previous to them. That generation will full on face the beast who is like a leopard, like a bear, like a lion, like the dragon. That generation will be in trial to choose to go food-less, water-less, shelter-less and head-less, dying *"for the word of God (Rev. 6:9),"* over the mark, or the name of the beast, or the number of his name (Rev. 6:9-11; 7:13-17; 13:2,16; 16:8; 20:4).

Should the Lord tarry, this generation will not be held accountable to the trial of that generation and the eternal death sentence their trial carries:

If any man worship the beast and his image, and receive his mark in his forehead, or in his hand, The same shall drink of the wine of the wrath of God, which is poured out without mixture into the cup of his indignation; and he shall be tormented with fire and brimstone in the presence of the holy angels, and in the presence of the Lamb: And the smoke of their torment ascendeth up for ever and ever: and they have no rest day nor night, who worship the beast and his image, and whosoever receiveth the mark of his name (Rev. 14:9-11)

Likewise, this *"church of the Laodiceans"* generation will be held accountable to trials that past generations were not held to the standard of, namely, the King James Bible, the finished word of God, inherited from *"the church in Philadelphia"* generation. In this generation, English speakers will be held to a higher standard of accountability than foreign language speakers. Furthermore, the leaders of God's people in the English leading portion of the church will be held to the highest of all standards to the very utmost.

For hundreds of years, when a soul declared faith that God wrote the Bible, they were declaring faith in the King James Bible. To the world, "Bible" intrinsically meant "The King James Bible." The tares of Satan were planted but had not harvested. It was not a trial for that generation, nor the generations before them.

Today, the Satanic harvest of counterfeit Bibles has come in like a pack of wolves in sheep's clothing to devour the flock. Can you imagine God saying, *"I never knew you: depart from me, ye that work iniquity (Matt. 7:23),"* because in Jesus' name you waged war against God's finished Bible before the world? How shameful! Or because in Jesus' name you belittled its supremacy and exclusivity before the little lambs? How negligent! Or because in Jesus' name you denied its authority in the church? How dishonorable! Do you really believe it is a small thing to throw out the KJV from the church? Be reminded of Rev. 3:20, *"Behold, I stand at the door, and knock."*

There will certainly be no claiming exemption on that day by comparing oneself to another, as in "Why am I being held accountable to this standard and my neighbor is not???" Comparing one generation to another generation, or comparing one's self to another neighbor, or comparing an English speaker to another tongue, for release of culpability, is total ignorance and foolishness. Put no hope in the fact that you were put to the test in what another was not. We are the English speaking leading office, leading grace, portion of the church assigned to keep the living oracle of God, and we are the generation that must accept full responsibility, liability and guilt for our actions regarding this word of God oracle, the King James Bible.

On the other hand, what does it look like for the one who overcomes the trial of thrones regarding the KJV finished word of God? It will look like suffering followed by perfect fruit.

First, consider this: it is only fitting for the true Bible to be rejected by men when you consider how much the Christian life revolves around being rejected by men.

Consequently, it is only fitting for the true Bible to bring you into its place of being rejected by men. Many will attempt to believe the King James Bible until this stage:

Yet hath he not root in himself, but dureth for a while: for when tribulation or persecution ariseth because of the word, by and by he is offended (Matt. 13:21)

As a result, you will need to go with Jesus alone for fruit bearing purposes:

But that on the good ground are they, which in an honest and good heart, having heard the word, keep it, and bring forth fruit with patience (Luke 8:15)

Notice that this Luke 8:15 verse regarding those who bear fruit uses the phrasing *"having heard the word, keep it"* and *"fruit with patience."* These are the same two wordings that Jesus commended *"the church in Philadelphia"* for, the prophetic church that finished the King James Bible, *"For thou... hast kept my word (Rev. 3:8)"* and *"Thou hast kept the word of my patience (Rev. 3:10)."*

God has set the gold standard for fruit bearing to be produced out of the "1611 King James Holy Bible." It is common knowledge that 9 is the official number in the Bible for *"fruit"* bearing (examples: the 9 *"fruit"* of the Spirit in Gal. 5:22,23; the 9 gifts of the Spirit in 1 Cor. 4:8-10).

1611 = 9 (1+6+1+1), King James = 9 letters, Holy Bible = 9 letters, together = 999, which is the ultimate expression in the Bible for bearing *"fruit."* The term *"be fruitful"* appears exactly 9 times in the King James Bible.

In due season, you will bear perfect fruit. You can never bear perfect fruit if you have not believed on the King James Bible. No matter how much you have matured in the Lord, you will always lack that critical belief from God's view point. You may admire your fruit more than God does, having missed this main issue in the trial of thrones during this Laodicean church hour.

CHAPTER 32

THE STANDARD LOWERED

WHEN THE ENEMY SHALL COME IN LIKE A FLOOD, THE SPIRIT OF THE LORD SHALL LIFT UP A STANDARD AGAINST HIM

ISAIAH 59:19

This chapter is very straight forward, sharp, and to the point: the church took down God's standard, which are the command and very words, *"there shall be no sodomite (Deut. 23:17)"* when they took down the King James Bible. This loosed in the world a flood of sodomites, transgenders, lesbians, transvestites, queers, the very host of abominations and the exceedingly wicked of sinners in our day in the most land mark and unprecedented way (Gen. 13:13/Lev. 18:22).

We will see this specifically through the expository exegesis of Isaiah fifty-nine; Isaiah fifty-nine's relationship to Ephesians six; Isaiah fifty-nine's relationship to Genesis nineteen; Isaiah fifty-nine's relationship to Deuteronomy twenty-three.

Perhaps no section of scripture is more popular than *"the armour of God (Ephesians 6)."* This is every man's favorite:

Put on the whole armour of God, that ye may be able to stand against the wiles of the devil. For we wrestle not against flesh and blood, but against principalities, against powers, against the rulers of the darkness of this world, against spiritual wickedness in high places (Eph. 6:11,12)

The procession of *"the armour of God"* comes next:

Stand therefore, having your loins girt about with truth, and having on the breastplate of righteousness; And your feet shod with the preparation of the gospel of peace; Above all, taking the shield of faith… And take the helmet of salvation, and the sword of the Spirit, which is the word of God (vs. 14-17)

The context of Isaiah fifty-nine is God's people beaten down and separated from God by their iniquities and their sins in the days of the kings. Weakened by the flood of evil and unable to effect salvation, God takes it upon Himself to form fit and bear *"the armour of God"* to be the standard raised up to save.

The Apostle Paul, who wrote Ephesians six, has drawn out three of the provisions of *"the armour of God"* from Isaiah fifty-nine. The first two are obvious enough:

For he put on righteousness as a breastplate, and an helmet of salvation upon his head (Isa. 59:17)

Compare with:

…and having on the breastplate of righteousness… And take the helmet of salvation… (Eph. 6:14,17)

The third provision of *"the armour of God"* from Isaiah fifty-nine is not as obvious:

When the enemy shall come in like a flood, the Spirit of the LORD shall lift up a standard against him (Isa. 59:19)

Based on Paul's supplement in the Ephesians 6 list of *"the armour of God,"* the Spirit of the Lord lifts the sword of the Lord, which is the Bible:

...and having on the breastplate of righteousness... And take the helmet of salvation, and the sword of the Spirit, which is the word of God (Eph. 6:14,17)

"The word of God" is the *"sword of the Spirit"* which means the Bible is the *"standard"* of *"the Spirit of the Lord"* in this Isaiah fifty-nine pre cursor of the Ephesians six armour of God. Lower the sword of the Spirit, lower the standard of the Spirit, let the enemy in like a flood.

When the standard is not raised, there is no defense against spiritual disease swarms. Isaiah fifty-nine delineates on this one by one, describing murder, lying, perverseness, vanity, poisonous youth, violence, promiscuity resulting in abortion, etc. Toward the end of this spectrum is total darkness, which is where sodomites abound:

We grope for the wall like the blind, and we grope as if we had no eyes: we stumble at noonday as in the night; we are in desolate places as dead men (Isa. 59:10)

The clause, *"We grope for the wall like the blind (Isa. 59:10),"* is the pointing of the Spirit to Isaiah fifty-nine's relationship to Genesis nineteen.

In Genesis nineteen we read of the angels who came as men to rescue Lot from the depravity of Sodom before the Lord rained brimstone and fire out of heaven upon it. Men consumed by their sexual lust for other men attempted to gang rape the angels who Lot took into his home. When the sodomites came near to break the door, the angels cast blindness to stop them:

And they smote the men that were at the door of the house with blindness, both small and great; so that they wearied themselves to find the door (Gen. 19:11)

Isaiah 59:10 and Genesis 19:11 are the only two places in the entire Bible that picture the blind reaching or groping or wearying for anything. Compare them:

We grope for the wall like the blind (Isa. 59:10)

Blindness... so that they wearied themselves to find the door (Gen. 19:11)

When the standard of the Bible is not lifted, sodomy cannot be stopped. This revelation of the Spirit is further supported by the fuller word of God as the historical context of Isaiah fifty-nine is occurring in the days of the kings:

And there were also sodomites in the land: and they did according to all the abominations of the nations which the LORD cast out before the children of Israel (1 Kings 14:24)

And he took away the sodomites out of the land, and removed all the idols that his fathers had made (1 Kings 15:12)

And the remnant of the sodomites, which remained in the days of his father Asa, he took out of the land (1 Kings 22:46)

And he brake down the houses of the sodomites, that were by the house of the LORD, where the women wove hangings for the grove (2 Kings 23:7)

This was so in the days of the kings, which were the days of Isaiah fifty-nine, and it is so in our day. The standard of the Spirit of the Lord which is the finished King James Bible is no longer lifted and the LGBTQ has come in like a flood.

Now we see Isaiah fifty-nine's relationship also to Deuteronomy twenty-three. When the bait of counterfeit Bibles was received by the church, the standard was lowered through deception, and when the KJV came down the single word *"sodomite"* came down with it. This word had been established by God against the enemy as a spiritual blockade in the heavenlies *"against spiritual wickedness in high places (Eph. 6:12)."* There is no other Bible that dares to use the word *"sodomite"* apart from the KJV:

There shall be no whore of the daughters of Israel, nor a sodomite of the sons of Israel (Deut. 23:17)

The command of the Lord out of His mouth, *"There shall be no sodomite (Deut. 23:17)"* was taken down by the church and replaced with Bibles that are stripped of the standard that the Spirit of the Lord had lifted. Evidence that they are counterfeit Bibles is seen in that they have no power to stop the LGBTQ invasion.

Satan did not build up a rampart, the church opened the door. The corporate church, and leadership most specifically, is responsible for the radical LGBTQ advancement of our day for abandoning the King James Bible and will be held responsible. If the standard of every word which has proceeded out of the mouth of God is lowered, all your preaching is in vain.

CHAPTER 33

COUNTERFEITS

FOR THEY CAST DOWN EVERY MAN HIS ROD, AND THEY BECAME SERPENTS: BUT AARON'S ROD SWALLOWED UP THEIR RODS

EXODUS 7:12

The Bible industrial complex will never bow down to the word of God King James Bible, until Jesus destroys it at the very end. Like Pharaoh of Egypt using the resource of God's people to support and build a worldly kingdom in the day of Moses and Aaron, the grip on money maker Bible translations is tight unto the same purpose.

Notwithstanding the mass marketing push that other Bibles are equal in authenticity or better in accuracy or readability to the King James Bible, there is only one rod of God in His hand and not many (Rev. 5:1). This rod is the King James Bible and not a counterfeit rod of the magicians of Pharaoh. God's rod carries the "authority" and "authenticity" and "authorship" of the "author" with His "authorization," and will devour the serpent imposter Bibles in God's timing:

When Pharaoh shall speak unto you, saying, Shew a miracle for you: then thou shalt say unto Aaron, Take thy rod, and cast it before Pharaoh, and it shall become a serpent (Ex. 7:9)

You, the reader, have been shown many miracles regarding the King James Bible in this book, of which are only the beginning of the unsearchable miracles of the authorized version of the word of God (John 20:30; 21:25). Regarding many of these miracles and wonders and signs, you may have said in your heart that the other Bible versions do them as well. Up to a point, you are right. That is the nature of a counterfeit, to copy in a lookalike manner:

Then Pharaoh also called the wise men and the sorcerers: now the magicians of Egypt, they also did in like manner with their enchantments. For they cast down every man his rod, and they became serpents (Ex. 7:11)

Because the overall sketch and outline of Bible versions are to pattern themselves after and follow the King James Version, a number of anomalies on the broader edge are duplicated, but none can carry on as the authorized version, and quickly give way to their ingenuine nature and lack of divine power and dominion:

but Aaron's rod swallowed up their rods (Ex. 7:11)

That the *"rod"* stands for the authority of God is undisputable. That the Bible stands for God's authority is also undisputable. That counterfeit rods, in the form of counterfeit Bibles, will be raised against the true rod of God is furthermore undisputable. Notice that in the New Testament, God re-announces Pharaoh's craft magicians whom confronted Moses' God given authority, this time in the church, even disclosing their names:

Now as Jannes and Jambres withstood Moses, so do these also resist the truth: men of corrupt minds, reprobate concerning the faith (2 Tim. 3:8)

By revealing their names, it is revealed that this is a vivid personal and forceful opposition to be dealt with by the church. The Jannes and Jambres of our day are named NIV, TNIV, NASB, ESV, NKJV, RSV, NRSV, NLT,

ASV, The New World Translation, The Amplified Bible, The Recovery Version Bible, The Living Bible, The Message Bible, etc., etc.; ad-nauseam.

God's work in the King James Bible is brought into discredit by man's imitation works and the church is robbed of power. This same 2 Timothy chapter three that exposes Pharaoh's magicians by name, is written to describe the last days experience of the church we are in:

This know also, that in the last days perilous times shall come. For men shall be lovers of their own selves, covetous, boasters, proud, blasphemers, disobedient to parents, unthankful, unholy, Without natural affection, trucebreakers, false accusers, incontinent, fierce, despisers of those that are good, Traitors, heady, highminded, lovers of pleasures more than lovers of God; Having a form of godliness, but denying the power thereof: from such turn away... Ever learning, and never able to come to the knowledge of the truth. Now as Jannes and Jambres withstood Moses, so do these also resist the truth: men of corrupt minds, reprobate concerning the faith. But they shall proceed no further: for their folly shall be manifest unto all men, as theirs also was (2 Tim. 3:1-5, 7-9)

Paul's reproof for this generation that will suffer the bad fruit of Bibles which are *"having a form of godliness, but denying the power thereof (vs. 5)"* is plain. The antidote for the beginning of 2 Timothy chapter three, is the end of 2 Timothy chapter three. There, Paul puts forth the *"rod"* of God to oppose the modern day Jannes and Jambres:

All scripture is given by inspiration of God, and is profitable for doctrine, for reproof, for correction, for instruction in righteousness: That the man of God may be perfect, throughly furnished unto all good works (2 Tim. 3:16)

We see Jannes and Jambres going up against the rod of God in this 2 Timothy chapter the same as we saw them opposing the rod of God in the Exodus chapter. This is an intentional match in the finished Bible and a repeated showdown, for an Old Testament/New Testament witness. Counterfeit Bibles, *"rods,"* look alike but *"resist the truth (vs. 8)"* of God's Bible, the authorized *"rod."*

In the course of reading this book you may have further said in your heart that you know many wonderful Christians who were saved and have grown reading other Bible translations. You may have said that they do not receive the King James Bible as the inspired word of God but embrace many Bible translations.

But how do you really know these individuals are truly saved souls? Most people simply assume that such individuals are saved because they are our friends and family and church leaders. However, do you know their walk twenty, thirty, forty years from now? This is not to say that they are not saved because they do not receive the KJV as God's finished Bible, nor to say that we should not receive them in the body of Christ for this reason, but simply to say that you truly do not know, do you?

When Moses put forth the rod of God and freed Israel from the rods of Pharaoh, the group making exodus was not all and entirely true converted souls, though surely, they would have thought so regarding one another since they were all walking away from Egypt and Pharaoh together:

And a mixed multitude went up also with them; and flocks, and herds, even very much cattle (Ex. 12:38)

We too might view the Exodus as having been all of God's genuine people since they staked a claim to depart from the world (Egypt) and Satan (Pharaoh), but the truth was,*"they are not all Israel, which are of Israel (Rom. 9:6)."* Likewise, we see the church as all of God's genuine people, but He sees a *"mixed multitude (Ex. 12:38)"* today, even as He did in the day of Israel's exodus.

In due time after the exodus, God exposed Israel's true from false through trial and test and He warns the same today in the church. In between the counterfeit Bibles of Jannes and Jambres producing the counterfeit Christians at the beginning of 2 Timothy chapter three, and the genuine God breathed *"scripture (vs. 3:16)"* producing the true *"man of God (vs. 17)"* at the end of 2 Timothy chapter three, are these words in the middle of the chapter:

> *But evil men and seducers shall wax worse and worse, deceiving, and being deceived (2 Tim. 3:13)*

When given light and opportunity to embrace the truth of God's true Bible, how do these individuals who embrace many spurious Bibles respond? Do they hear the shepherd's voice? *"A stranger will they not follow… my sheep hear my voice (John 10:5,27)."* Do they harden their heart in unbelief? *"For we which have believed do enter into rest (Heb. 4:3)."* Do they ridicule and belittle and outsmart the truth? *"…even to them which stumble at the word, being disobedient: whereunto also they were appointed (1 Pet. 2:8)."* Is this good fruit?

It's not how one starts their walk with Christ it's how one finishes, and to not acknowledge, or worse, to disavow God's finished Bible, is a pretty bad start, let alone finish. It does not matter how popular you are in the world of Christianity or how many people are wrapped around you in a fancy church denomination, building, seminary, college, or ministry program by television, radio or internet. Finishing famous in the public eye is not the goal we are to aim for, *"For do I now persuade men, or God? or do I seek to please men? for if I yet pleased men, I should not be the servant of Christ (Gal. 1:10)."* The goal is truth in our inward parts, *"…for the LORD seeth not as man seeth; for man looketh on the outward appearance, but the LORD looketh on the heart (1 Sam. 16:7)."*

And if these people who embrace many Bible versions with infidelity to God's finished Bible are saved souls, does this change the truth? Or Should we continue in the error of their way? Or should we settle for mediocrity regarding our own accuracy on account of them? Or shall we judge the truth according to ourselves rather than the word of God, and base what is true on ourselves rather than on the word of God? In other words, if the whole church does wrong, shall we also?

> *For we dare not make ourselves of the number, or compare ourselves with some that commend themselves: but they measuring themselves by themselves, and comparing themselves among themselves, are not wise (2 Cor. 10:12)*

The day of God's judgment will be staggered, and what one man will be judged for, another will not. One man will never have heard of the King James Bible nor judged the more for it. Another man will ruin his entire ministry from his steadfast defiance to God's Holy Bible. Some will have built on the foundation of Jesus Christ with gold, silver, precious stones. Some will have built on the foundation of Jesus Christ with wood, hay, stubble. Will you take chance in such a matter as important to God as His finished Bible?

The truth of the matter is that we will only know the untold damage of the counterfeit Bible rebellion when we leave the stage and pass through the other side of the curtain into eternity. How many turned away from Christ because of the schizophrenia of English Bibles? How many read and read and read and gained no power of conversion from dead Bibles? How many trifled the Bible since there was no standard and lost reward? How many will be guilty of many lovers by playing the Bible whore, no differently than Israel, *"I will go after my lovers, that give me my bread (Hosea 2:5)."*

For now, we should see the 2 Timothy chapter three anemic condition of the church in our day which is deprived of the King James Bible, and the Holy Ghost link with Jannes and Jambres and their counterfeit rods. By this let us take extreme warning.

Also, for now, it is sufficient for us to know that Satan has a better understanding and perspective of the eternal ruin caused by the counterfeit Bible rebellion than we do, and if it's important to him, it's of very serious implication to both Christ and the church.

Chapter 34

Preference Or Conviction?

> And Elijah came unto all the people, and said, How long halt ye between two opinions? If the LORD be God, follow him: but if Baal, then follow him. And the people answered him not a word
>
> 1 Kings 18:21

God hates a weak man.

The following are traits of a weak man: Godless; Christless, Spiritless; wordless; thoughtless; gutless; conditioned; unreasonable; rash; uncorrectable; unteachable; dull; passive; shallow; indifferent; indecisive; ineffective; lazy; cannot take charge; a slave of the world; in bonds to the flesh; caves in to the soul; serves the Devil; blames others; fears men; fears women even more; a man who hides; a man who compromises; a man who cannot suffer; a man without conviction; void of truth.

Such a man can never come to the conclusion that God has finished a Bible, let alone stand for it. It will cost more than he has to give. The above described man will at best come to the conclusion that the King James

Bible is a very good translation. Perhaps, he may even stretch to say that the King James Bible is his preferred translation.

Both of these positions, "the King James Bible is a fine translation" and "I prefer the King James translation myself" leave the weak man a back door to equivocate in any circumstance necessary. Amongst the church he looks like a real Bible believer. To the world he can still dismount quickly from any certain idea that there is such thing as an inspired living Bible. To the church he looks religious and to the world he looks intellectual. Both of these positions are soft options, which ease pressure and persecution.

However, acknowledging the validity or preference of the King James Bible among translations is not faith. Only conviction will count as faith, and only conviction will please God, and only conviction will result in reward. A good translation… or the scriptures? Your preference… or the perfect word of God?

Believing in the concept of a verbal, plenary, inspired Bible and actually claiming one on the Earth are the difference between make believe and reality:

Even so faith, if it hath not works, is dead, being alone (James 2:17)

To apply the spirit of this verse in application to bibliology, would be the likes of this:

Even so faith that the Bible is of verbal plenary inspiration, if it hath not that verbal plenary inspired Bible, is dead, being alone (James 2:17)

This verse which discerns between true faith and a sham continues:

Yea, a man may say, Thou hast faith, and I have works: shew me thy faith without thy works, and I will shew thee my faith by my works (James 2:18)

Again, the spirit of this verse in application to bibliology:

Yea, a man may say, Thou hast faith in the verbal plenary inspiration of the Bible, and I actually have a verbal plenary inspired Bible: show me your faith in a verbal plenary inspired Bible without actually having one, and I will show you my faith in a verbal plenary inspired Bible by my King James Bible (James 2:18)

God is preparing men and women to stand before Him in precision, by faith in Jesus Christ, by the word of God, in the heavenly courts, temple and throne, before the redeemed counsels of prophets and saints and the holy angels. For those who are coming to know, it is time to believe the truth.

To the weak men who resist and suppress the truth, such praise of the King James Bible amongst translations and preference of the King James Bible amongst versions is an insult to God and dead faith without works.

CHAPTER 35

BABEL

> THEREFORE IS THE NAME OF IT CALLED
> BABEL; BECAUSE THE LORD DID
> THERE CONFOUND THE LANGUAGE
> OF ALL THE EARTH
>
> GENESIS 11:9

At the very least, Satan has used the mass distribution of counterfeit Bibles to ravage the church in the end of days: dilution and dissimilation of Bible translations has weakened and fractured the unity around the truth and the cohesiveness of the body of Christ.

The following is to make a point regarding the church gathering experience and Bible translations:

> Christian #1: "Everyone turn to Matthew 9:13, '*for I am not come to call the righteous, but sinners to repentance (KJV)*'"

> Christian #2: "My Bible doesn't say you have to repent (ESV)"

> Christian #1: "Ok, then let's turn to Matthew 18:11, '*For the Son of man is come to save that which was lost (KJV)*'"

Christian #3: "My Bible foot notes say this verse shouldn't even be in the Bible (NASB). Are you sure you know what you are teaching?"

Christian #1: "Ok, Ok, let's just turn to Mark 11:26, *But if ye do not forgive, neither will your Father which is in heaven forgive your trespasses (KJV)*"

Christian #4: "My Bible doesn't even have that verse in it (NIV). My Bible just skips from verse 25 to verse 27. What's wrong with this Bible?"

Christian #5: "Hey, I am a baby Christian. What's going on with all these different Bibles??"

Unbeliever #1: "Thanks for inviting me to this Bible study but you guys need to get your act together. See you later!"

Do you really believe that God has left His Bible ambiguous like this and in sordid condition, with doubtful passages and even holes? With question after question as to authenticity and accuracy of content and expression? With no final authoritative edition anywhere on the face of the earth? Do you believe He has dealt to the church no differently then He dealt to Satan at the tower of Babel? What do I mean by this?

Satan long ago made a promise to Eve of immortality and god like production, *"Ye shall not surely die... ye shall be as gods (Gen. 3:4,5)."*

In the path and labor of fulfilling this ancient promise to Eve, came the first world order of the kingdom and tower of Babel through the anti-christ prefigure of Nimrod (Genesis 11:1-9).

The world had the strength and common force of one language at that time. However, God massively stunted the traction of Satan's one world order by confounding language and forking all tongues. Satan, who sowed this same seed in Genesis chapter three when he forked the first Bible translation (refer back to chapter three of this book), had now reaped the seed he planted there upon his own head, *"Be not deceived; God is not mocked: for whatsoever a man soweth, that shall he also reap (Gal. 6:7)."* At the tower of Babel, Satan experienced self-ward in full scale the power and effect of the confusion that arises from communication breakdown.

Literally speaking, this is Satan's oldest trick in the book. Eve had fallen for it. And now the church, whom Eve is a prophetic picture of, has fallen for it, *"Lest Satan should get an advantage of us: for we are not ignorant of his devices (2 Cor. 2:11)."* Eve succumbed in the beginning in Genesis and the church has succumbed in the end in Revelation.

Satan has dished back to the church of God that which was dished out to him by God at the tower of Babel. Scarcely hindered now by the confused church, seduced to put down the actual word of God which has proceeded out of God's very own mouth, Satan continues his venture to the final New World Order of the anti-christ in our day, which is the completion of the tower and kingdom of Babel. He is doing this with a full rush and at exponentially increasing speed: Apple, Amazon, Micro Soft, Google, Wal-Mart, Martial Law, 911, FEMA, NSA, UN, EU, CFR, Trilateral Commission, Bilderberg, Illuminati, Gender Reassignment, Transhumanism, CERN, Singularity, Nano Tech, AI, Vaccines, GMO, Chemtrails, DUMBS, UFO, MK Ultra, Predictive Programming, Hegelian Dialectic, Disinformation, Perception Without Awareness; *"Woe to the inhabiters of the earth and of the sea! for the devil is come down unto you, having great wrath, because he knoweth that he hath but a short time (Rev. 12:12)."*

Even as God has given Satan a temporary victory in the original fall of man in the beginning, we know clearly that the entire tone of the last days will also be God giving Satan another temporary victory, *"And it was given unto him to make war with the saints, and to overcome them (Rev. 13:7)."* Just as in the Genesis 3 expose, the true words of God out of his mouth had to be removed in order to give way for Satan to have a victory, so must it be in the end. Satan can never have the victory while God's word which proceeds out of His mouth stands. Counterfeit Bibles do not proceed out of the mouth of God. Satan knows this. Do you?

Be sure that God is allowing this state of affairs in the church regarding the unbelief, disrespect, defaming and trampling of the King James Bible in accordance with His wisdom. As said back in chapter ten of this book, because of the usefulness of counterfeit Bibles it is not God's will to remove them today but instead to preserve you from them as you grow.

God's mandated way is not to remove the trouble but to make you an overcomer above it (Rev. 2:7,11,17,26; 3:5,12,21; 21:7). It is God's way in Christ today and has always been His way to prove His people through the presence of an enemy. In the day of the conquest of Joshua and the children of Israel into the promised land, God intentionally raised enemies to occupy the land before, during and after Joshua. God insisted He would not remove these enemies but that they were to do it by overcoming them:

> *Wherefore I also said, I will not drive them out from before you; but they shall be as thorns in your sides, and their gods shall be a snare unto you (Judges 2:3)*

Overcoming was the only way out for Joshua and the children of Israel. The only way out was to go through. There would be no sharing of the land with the enemy. The church is given no less an option. The Apostle Paul recites this Judges 2:3 verse and is rebuked by Jesus that he must overcome that which He intends not to take away, as Paul pressed on to occupy Christ the land as his spiritual sphere to dwell in as an overcomer:

> *…there was given to me a thorn in the flesh, the messenger of Satan to buffet me, lest I should be exalted above measure. For this thing I besought the Lord thrice, that it might depart from me. And he said unto me, My grace is sufficient for thee: for my strength is made perfect in weakness. Most gladly therefore will I rather glory in my infirmities, that the power of Christ may rest upon me (2 Cor. 12:7-9)*

Compare what God said with Paul's cry:

> *…they shall be as thorns in your sides… (Judges 2:3)*

> *…there was given to me a thorn in the flesh… (2 Cor. 12:7)*

Returning to the continuation of the Judges chapter and versing, God revealed in the end His motives in this kind of practice:

And the anger of the LORD was hot against Israel; and he said, Because that this people hath transgressed my covenant which I commanded their fathers, and have not hearkened unto my voice; I also will not henceforth drive out any from before them of the nations which Joshua left when he died: That through them I may prove Israel, whether they will keep the way of the LORD to walk therein, as their fathers did keep it, or not. Therefore the LORD left those nations, without driving them out hastily; neither delivered he them into the hand of Joshua (Judges 2:20-23)

Our fathers have kept the way of the Lord regarding the finished Bible, God's voice, for nearly four hundred years. We are the generation after them and we have forsaken the Bible of our fathers for contending manmade Bibles, and this in the name of money at the root.

The Zondervans of the world will never stop printing Babel Bibles to deceive, but God's grace within you will cause you to overcome the Bible translation lies if you truly want to know. God has left them for you to throw out by the power of Christ that you may be proved.

CHAPTER 36

FIRST THE NATURAL THEN THE SPIRITUAL

> HOWBEIT THAT WAS NOT FIRST WHICH IS SPIRITUAL, BUT THAT WHICH IS NATURAL; AND AFTERWARD THAT WHICH IS SPIRITUAL
>
> 1 CORINTHIANS 15:46

Most people will not have read this far in the book. If you have read this far, you must really want to know the truth. Others will reach this chapter by lightly approaching God in the matter, by peeking into chapters or skimming through in a curious but aloof or perhaps arrogant way.

In either case, God has been waiting for a very long time for you, perhaps decades as a devout Christian, to acknowledge His perfect Bible, by grace through faith, for what it is, the heart of the Father, the character of the Father, and the perfection of the Son, to be judged by no man.

Whether you are the one who has intently read straight through with conviction, or the one who has cherry picked in a spirit of unbelief, there is no telling which of you will be caught by Jesus in the end, in this all-important matter. We are reminded of Jesus' words:

But what think ye? A certain man had two sons; and he came to the first, and said, Son, go work to day in my vineyard. He answered and said, I will not: but afterward he repented, and went. And he came to the second, and said likewise. And he answered and said, I go, sir: and went not. Whether of them twain did the will of his father? (Matt. 21:28-31)

Why does it take so long, in most cases, to embrace the truth of the King James Bible as the very word of God? And why do so many who do believe from the beginning of their walk tend to fall away to other Bibles down the way? And why in so many cases, is there such hostility and anger and even rage in professing Christians toward the idea that the King James Bible is alone, the very Bible from God? When I share the miracles and wonders and signs, which God did by the KJV, time and time again, I can see the massive disappointment in the countenance of Christians, at the chance that God has actually finished a Bible and will accept no others.

Again, why is this? The direct answer is: *"But the natural man receiveth not the things of the Spirit of God: for they are foolishness unto him: neither can he know them, because they are spiritually discerned (1 Cor. 2:14)."*

It is the natural principal to first believe that God has not written the Bible. All evidence reaffirms this belief because the natural man has a dark decision already in place. All evidence is selected and rejected based on protecting this dark decision, therefore, to him, God has not written the Bible.

Even the Christian must pass through the next layer of the natural principal which is a part of the nature of his old man. While the dark decision in his heart has been overturned and he now believes in the concept that God wrote the Bible, there is still a deep decision in his heart and an abiding in the naturalness of his mind against the true Bible itself which God has actually written and finished. He has not recognized yet, that he believes out of his own natural strength that God wrote the Bible. Therefore, he has countless natural and academic reasons why the KJV is not God's finished Bible, yet, neither can he recognize any specific Bible either, which he dares to confess is from above to the exclusion of all others. At this point he believes God wrote the Bible but there is no actual Bible which God has written that he knows of. The natural man hedges toward the truth but the truth is really in another realm, the Spirit realm, so he can never grasp it. It is a phantom concept to the natural man and therefore nothing he can lay hold of in the actual sense.

In both natural cases, the unbeliever and the Christian, the mind of the flesh is deterministic. Before thought in the matter honestly occurs in the heart of hearts, it has a dark or deep decision already in place. This decision is according to what the self wants or what the self doesn't want. Through thinking by the power of the natural man, the will, controlled by the "want" or "doesn't want" of the self, is then made manifest according to its pre-determination. In other words, thinking the matter through, such as contemplating this book, does not change anything, but is a covering and a steering for the bias of the soul and will only manifest its predetermined way. The unbeliever needs Jesus to save him to begin with, and the Christian needs Jesus to save him from start to finish. It is in between the start and finish that the Spirit must deal with the natural man in order to render the Christian truly spiritual. Only then will he see God's true Bible.

In the case of those who begin their walk embracing the King James Bible as the word of God, only to eventually turn away to embrace other Bibles that are not from God, similarly, the natural man cannot continue to the end to uphold the truth of God. This requires the spiritual man who has had his naturalness dealt with by the Spirit and the cross. In this sense, though he showed a good start outwardly, he was no different than the unbeliever and the Christian example in the aforementioned paragraph. The natural man is the natural man no matter how good he starts off, and cannot meet the demands of God Almighty, which in this case, is to believe unto the end on the word of God, even His finished Bible, the King James Authorized Version.

In the case of the hostile ones that flair up or possibly rage at the insistence that God has finished the KJV Bible, of course all the above is also true. The reaction of their natural man with strong antagonism toward the idea of the exclusive authority of the King James Bible is actually proof that they are stumbling over the true Bible, *"Because the carnal mind is enmity against God: for it is not subject to the law of God, neither indeed can be. So then they that are in the flesh cannot please God (Rom. 8:7,8)."* Their experience is much like the pre-condition of the Apostle Paul who was enraged with the audacity of the church and was a destroyer of the body of Christ in ignorance:

Who was before a blasphemer, and a persecutor, and injurious: but I obtained mercy, because I did it ignorantly in unbelief (1 Timothy 1:13)

Of course, this was before Paul was regenerated, so it is never a good sign to vehemently denounce or kill the things of God, especially His word, the King James Bible, even if it is by ignorance in unbelief. Scoffer beware, as this symptom in you may be revealing you are yet to be regenerated (born again) despite your steadfast insistence to the contrary.

In line with this understanding that the natural man believes first in the concept that God wrote the Bible before ever knowing which one it is, we have similar understanding regarding our affairs with Satan, the god of this world. It is first for us to be deceived by Satan in the world before we ever see the light of Christ as our salvation. Our natural man must first have its way of all of its lusts, for the natural course of this world, through the deception of the evil one. This includes all of our religious attempts to bring forth "Ishmaels" in order to help God. Only then can we truly come to Christ for a true spiritual walk in Him according to who He is. Likewise, regarding God's finished Bible, it is first for us to be deceived by Satan through our natural man with the many counterfeits presented, then to overcome through faith. Not the other way around. First the natural stumbling, then the spiritual overcoming.

There is only one defense from Satan preying on your natural man, and God has only one solution for the natural man that keeps us from believing the truth, and that is, that all of him, the natural man, must go to the cross. In all of these cases cited, God is waiting for the natural man to finally expire. Only then will your own willingness agree with God to consign your natural man to the cross. Only then will you accompany God in His death blow to your natural man. Only then will you cease your warring against Him and all truth.

In all cases, the natural man must first be experienced and passed through, until you no longer care for your "self," then, to be done away with by the cross of Christ, before the spiritual man can emerge. Only the spiritual man will have eyes to see the Bible God finished because it is the epitome of spirituality. This order is God's way for all who are in Adam to be raised up in Christ:

> *Howbeit that was not first which is spiritual, but that which is natural; and afterward that which is spiritual (1 Cor. 15:46)*

Four verses later we are told…

> *Now this I say, brethren, that flesh and blood cannot inherit the kingdom of God; neither doth corruption inherit incorruption (vs. 50)*

"Flesh and blood" is the natural man, the remnant of the Adamic life, which will never see the Bible God has finished. Seeing the word of God is part and parcel of what it means to *"inherit the kingdom of God."* The natural man is of *"corruption"* and cannot *"inherit incorruption"* which is the pure word of God (Ps. 12:6), for all intents and purposes of this book.

The natural man must be replaced by the resurrected man now, not after this world, and that means the cross must come now and in this life time. This cross is not the theology of the cross, this cross is the experience of the cross. Even our Lord went this way in experience in order to take the natural man to the cross to be dealt death by the hand of the Father. He has commanded all who are of the truth to follow him:

> *Verily, verily, I say unto you, Except a corn of wheat fall into the ground and die, it abideth alone: but if it die, it bringeth forth much fruit. He that loveth his life shall lose it; and he that hateth his life in this world shall keep it unto life eternal (John 12:24,25)*

The *"corn of wheat"* must *"fall into the ground"* so its naturalness of shell will *"die"* and release the true life of the seed within. This is a form of resurrection and this is the way to *"bear much fruit."* Also see, Matt. 10:38,39; 16:24,25; Luke 9:23,24.

Our natural man must follow Jesus to the totality of its death. If we insist on protecting our natural man shell, which manifests our natural man thinking, from our natural man mind, by our natural man strength, we will never bear the fruit of God, including never believing in the finished Bible of God in our spirit by the Spirit.

CHAPTER 37

FOREIGN LANGUAGE BIBLES

IT SHALL COME, THAT I WILL GATHER ALL NATIONS AND TONGUES; AND THEY SHALL COME, AND SEE MY GLORY

ISAIAH 66:18

We speak English and we will be accountable to God for speaking English. The conditions of God, as per the responsibility of speaking English and the significance of the bible being finished in English, are upon us and not others.

We are not the world that needs translations of the Bible, we have the inspired word of God, but there is a world that does need translations of the Bible.

Truth be told, God's word is powerful in any language:

And they were all filled with the Holy Ghost, and began to speak with other tongues, as the Spirit gave them utterance (Acts 2:4)

The exception to this would be English if you are correcting God's English. In this case, such a translation will not be powerful but an infraction, as God cannot be improved upon.

To translate the Bible into a tongue of the nations that needs the Bible is merciful and kind and compassionate and a great act of charity unto those who are perishing. To re-translate God's inspired word out of His choice of English into your choice of English is ignorant and foolish and scandalous and a great act of independence.

Ignorance, foolishness, scandal, and independence will never lead you into rest, which is the end of the Christian faith (Gen. 2:2; Matt. 11:28, 29; Heb. 4:11; Rev. 14:11,13). Do you have a life of spiritual rest?

Perhaps you are young in either physical age or Christian spiritual age. In this case, you are more concerned with earthly fun than heavenly rest. However, the desire for earthly fun will be surpassed and the day will come once and forever when you will desire heavenly rest above all. Heavenly rest is for the mature. Heavenly rest is the accompaniment of the Father. Heavenly rest is divine.

It is not the Spirit of glory and rest (1 Pet. 4:14) but a works mindedness that breeds one English Bible translation after another with *"variance (Gal. 5:19-21)."* If you are still working out the English translation of the Bible by flip flopping between Bible translations or sourcing which English words are truly conveying the Hebrew and Greek, you are in unbelief. Like ignorance, foolishness, scandal, and independence, so also unbelief will deny you rest. You, in this condition, cannot enter the rest of God regarding the Bible. God is at rest regarding His finished Bible, but you are not joined with Him in this way.

Closely linked to divine rest is divine favor. The King James Bible is at rest for over four hundred years now and has no need to be re-translated for updating sake or any other sake because it is in the divine favor of God. If you personally do not bear the fruit of heavenly rest in your life you are lacking a measure of divine favor from the Father. Settling this matter of the true word of God and entering His rest in this crucial area will be a great step of entering divine rest out from unbelief and ceasing from all of your works of the fleshly mind.

While the King James Bible stands alone as the inspired word of God to be bowed to, a foreign language translation of the Bible is exactly that, a translation. The King James Bible is perfect, but a translation of the Bible into another language can be good or bad, for better or for worse.

To possess the King James Bible is absolute divine favor and brings rest to exactly what God has said, glorifying His name through your faith according to the act of His will which He has achieved by His Spirit. To possess a foreign translation of the Bible is a measure of divine favor but cannot be considered to be the level of the election of grace bestowed upon the KJV and those who embrace it as such. Foreign translations carry with them the truth like the thought of the Phoenician woman who said to Jesus, *"Truth, Lord: yet the dogs eat of the crumbs which fall from their masters' table (Matt. 15:27)."* Such is the economy of God regarding the special revelation of the Holy Bible. Some shall eat the whole of the loaf from the table and some shall eat the partial crumbs from under the table. All shall be thankful.

Foreign translations of the Bible are necessary for bringing in the gentiles, but they are not the inspired and inerrant final Bible of God sanctified in heaven. Rather, as *"crumbs which fall from the master's table,"* they reflect the strata of God's choosing, election and divine favor toward one man (the English speaker) over another (the foreign language speaker), in privilege and proximity to Himself. Originally, when the scriptures were in Hebrew, the seed of the Bible, God's choosing, election and divine favor, privilege and proximity to Himself was toward the Jews over the foreign language speaker: *"What advantage then hath the Jew? ...Much every way: chiefly, because that unto them were committed the oracles of God (Rom. 3:1,2)."* Today, this has been forfeited over by the Jews to the English-speaking portion of the world. Do not make their costly mistake!

Everywhere in the Bible we see this economy of God revealed from lesser to greater expressions of divine favor in privilege and proximity to Himself. There were the five thousand disciples whom Jesus fed (Matt. 14:21/Mark 6:44). Then there were the five hundred disciples whom Jesus showed Himself to in His resurrection (1 Cor. 15:6). Then there were the twelve disciples whom Jesus chose to accompany Him and to inherit apostleship (Matt. 10:1, 2). Then there were the three whom Jesus revealed His glory of deity to at the transfiguration (Mark 9:2). Then there was the one disciple who was bestowed with the honorable declaration four times as the *"disciple whom Jesus loved (John 13:23; 20:2; 21:7; 21:20)."* There is narrower divine favor, privilege and proximity yet, to Jesus alone, *"This is my beloved Son, in whom I am well pleased (Matt. 3:17)."*

We are all, worldwide, concluded in unbelief (Rom. 11:32). Unbelief in anything regarding the truth is all of our starting point and position and even our nature. We are all worldwide, beggars before God and desperate for the truth. From there we must all begin. Therefore, as English speakers, we are to be extremely thankful to God for any foreign language Bible that reaches the perishing world, no matter how good or bad, or for better or for worse, the translation may be. These foreign translation Bibles are supplying an eternal, life and death need of the special revelation of the gospel, and the bread of life, and the light to the gentiles, where there is an absolute void of such.

To those of us who are privileged to speak English, the language of the finished perfect Bible, we must be astute in understanding the personality of our God, who can very sharply acquit one where to another He will impute massive guilt. Do not lump yourself into a group, such as the world group, to justify your unbelief in His finished Bible, because God will be judging you as an individual. God will know if you hardened your heart to this truth. God will know if you lived lukewarm in the presence of the finished Bible. God will know if you suppressed the truth for your own personal ministry. God will know if you squandered the opportunity and forfeited your privilege like Israel did. One thing is safe to say, the longer we abide in the presence of opportunity and privilege the more the Master will expect from us and the more we will progress down the curve toward the imputation of guilt. And we are certainly a people and a generation of opportunity and privilege like no other: *"For unto whomsoever much is given, of him shall be much required: and to whom men have committed much, of him they will ask the more (Luke 12:48)."* Do not stop proceeding forward with God because another in the world, or in your church, has less than you in this matter. Run the race according to the truth despite those around you: *"For whosoever hath, to him shall be given, and he shall have more abundance: but whosoever hath not, from him shall be taken away even that he hath (Matt. 13:12)"* and *"…and unto you that hear shall more be given. For he that hath, to him shall be given: and he that hath not, from him shall be taken even that which he hath (Mark 4:24,25)."*

A final word regarding translations. I am sure the question still remains for some, "What about the New King James Version?" If you are still asking this then you have not comprehended the essence of this book. Let it be simple in Christ that whatever is not the King James Bible, is not the King James Bible. Be encouraged to read this book again as each time will bring valuable understanding that is deeper than, and was not gained, the time prior.

CHAPTER 38

BIOS

THE WORDS THAT I SPEAK UNTO YOU,
THEY ARE SPIRIT, AND THEY ARE LIFE

JOHN 6:63

We saw in chapters fifteen through twenty of this book that God made the Bible, the word of God, to be intentionally in the image and likeness of the human body, because *"the Word was made flesh (John 1:14)."*

We sampled but a selection of the attribute demonstrations which are carried by the King James Bible revealing the human body: the spiral DNA, the right side left side body paradigm, the right side dominate trait, the spine and vertebrae, the chromosomes, the rungs of DNA, the heart of the body, the blood of the body, the immune system of the body, the skin of the body, the hands and feet of the body, the stripes of the Lord Jesus upon His body, the tree His body hung upon, and the shedding of the bodily blood of the Lord Jesus Christ sprinkled and spotting the pages of the Bible.

We return to this subject one last time to conclude this book with a sampler journey through the genome of the Bible which is the book of the prophet Isaiah. Since the discovery of DNA, the field of genetics has leaped at the chance to create the perfect human being. A part of this conquest was a scientific research project known as the Human Genome Project which began in 1990 and was completed in 2003. Simply stated, the goal was to map every gene of the human genome.

God has done just such a thing in the King James Bible. Deep within the core of Isaiah is the identifying and mapping of all of the genes of the Bible, the very Bible genome, from both a linguistic and literary and functional standpoint. The result is the perfect man, Jesus Christ, the Word of God.

This genome book of Isaiah has a unique total of sixty-six chapters. The Bible as a whole also has a unique total of sixty-six books. Isaiah acts as the genome for the body of the Bible because each chapter contains identical matches in words, phrases and themes to each book of the Bible, in perfect chronological order, from beginning to end. This means that chapter one of Isaiah matches the book of Genesis, and chapter two of Isaiah matches the book of Exodus, and so on and so on, consecutively through to the last chapter of Isaiah and the last book of the Bible.

Isaiah itself, as the genome book of the Bible, is located appropriately enough as book number twenty-three in the divine lineup of the books of the Bible. This means, of course, that chapter twenty-three of Isaiah is about the book of Isaiah. That is twenty-three, two times. This matches the number of twenty-three chromosomes supplied by the patriarch and twenty-three chromosomes supplied by the matriarch in the new creation of a body. This is a genome factor.

For the following last four chapters of this book we will demonstrate the Isaiah genome of the Bible and its matured body, the finished King James Bible. Please understand that many of the Bible's authors such as Moses wrote their content before Isaiah lived. Likewise, Isaiah wrote before others lived and wrote their content, such as John. Still yet, all of the authors of the Bible were unaware of the coming order of the books, the chapters, the verses, the words, the letters, the numbers, and especially the King James Bible itself. The Holy Ghost is the only single author who has been involved from beginning to end as super intendent.

Please also understand that our goal in the following and final four chapters is strictly to sample from each chapter of Isaiah and the books of the Bible, the perfect miracle of Spirit and life as found in the King James Bible. There is no way to even begin saturating these miraculous examples without writing another entire book. This subject alone, the genome of the Bible, is truly an entire book all unto itself. The purpose then being that these samples will launch you into your own discovery of the King James Bible perfect word of God.

Because of the brevity of words that I will be using to marathon through the sixty-six chapters of Isaiah and the matching sixty-six books of the Bible, the readers familiarity with the scriptures will be heavily required from here on out. The deeper you know the scriptures the more you will be impressed. May God bless your faith.

That the trial of your faith, being much more precious than of gold that perisheth, though it be tried with fire, might be found unto praise and honour and glory at the appearing of Jesus Christ (1 Peter 1:7)

CHAPTER 39

IT IS FINISHED 1

JESUS SAITH UNTO THEM, MY MEAT IS TO DO THE WILL OF HIM THAT SENT ME, AND TO FINISH HIS WORK

JOHN 4:34

Isaiah chapter 1   Genesis book 1

Isaiah 1:2 Hear, O *heavens*, and give ear, O *earth*: for the LORD hath spoken, I have nourished and *brought up children, and they have rebelled against me*.

Genesis 2:1 Thus the *heavens* and the *earth* were finished, and all the host of them.

(special notes: Note how 1:2 and 2:1 mirror each other; next, compare *"brought up children, and they have rebelled against me"* from Isaiah chapter 1 with the creation and fall of Adam and Eve in Genesis book 1)

Isaiah 1:9 Except the LORD of hosts had left unto us a very small remnant, we should have been as *Sodom*, and we should have been like unto *Gomorrah*.

Genesis 19 God destroys *Sodom* and *Gomorrah*.

(special notes: Note how 1:9 and 19 are identical in number)

Isaiah 1:16 Wash you, make you *clean*; *put away* the evil of your doings from before mine eyes; cease to do evil;

Genesis 35:2 …*Put away* the strange gods that are among you, and be *clean*, and change your garments:

(special notes: Isaiah chapter 1 in match with Genesis book 1 are the only two places where the word *"put"* and *"away"* and *"clean"* are used in the same verse in the entire Bible KJV)

Isaiah chapter 2   Exodus book 2

Isaiah 2:3 And many people shall go and say, *Come* ye, and let us go *up to the mountain* of *the LORD*, to the house of the God of Jacob; and he will *teach us* of his ways,

Exodus 24:12 And *the LORD* said unto Moses, *Come up to* me into *the mount*, and be there: and I will give thee tables of stone, and a law, and commandments which I have written; that thou mayest *teach them*."

(special notes: Isaiah chapter 2 speaks of going up to the mountain of the LORD in verse 3, and Moses goes to the mountain of God for the first time in book 2 'Exodus' in chapter 3)

Isaiah 2:11 …the LORD alone shall be exalted

Isaiah 2:17 …the LORD alone shall be exalted

Exodus 20:3 Thou shalt have no other gods before me.

(special notes: the phrase "the LORD alone shall be exalted" occurs only in Isaiah 2 in match with the famous commandment from Exodus book 2 in the entire KJV)

Isaiah chapter 3   Leviticus book 3

Isaiah 3:1 For, behold, the Lord, *the LORD of hosts, doth take away* from Jerusalem and from Judah the stay and *the staff*, the whole stay *of bread*…

Leviticus 26:26 And when *I have broken the staff of your bread*…

(special notes: the words *"staff"* and *"bread"* only appear in the same verse together in the book of Isaiah in chapter 3 in match with Leviticus book 3 in the KJV)

Isaiah 3:17 Therefore the Lord will smite with a *scab* the crown of the head of the daughters of Zion…

Leviticus 13:7 But if the *scab* spread much abroad in the skin…

(special notes: the word *"scab"* only appears one time in the book of Isaiah. This occurrence is in Isaiah chapter 3 in match with Leviticus book 3 in the KJV; next, compare matching numbers 3:17 and 13:7)

Isaiah 3:24 And it shall come to pass, that *instead of sweet smell* there shall be stink; and instead of a *girdle* a rent;

Leviticus 8:7 And he put upon him the coat, and girded him with the *girdle*, and clothed him with the robe, and put the ephod upon him, and he girded him with the curious *girdle* of the ephod, and bound it unto him therewith.

Leviticus 26:31 …and I will *not smell the savour of your sweet odours*.

(special notes: there are 16 accounts in Leviticus of the priestly role of turning the stench of man into the *"sweet savour"* of Christ, as pictured in the offerings)

Isaiah chapter 4   Numbers book 4

Isaiah 4:5 And the LORD will create upon every dwelling place of mount Zion, and upon her assemblies, a *cloud* and smoke *by day, and* the shining of a flaming *fire by night:*

Numbers 9:16 So it was alway: the *cloud* covered it *by day, and* the appearance of *fire by night.*

Isaiah 4:6 And there shall be a *tabernacle* for a shadow in the daytime from the heat, and for a place of *refuge,*

Numbers 35:6 And among the cities which ye shall give unto the Levites there shall be six cities for *refuge,*

(special notes: the word *"tabernacle"* first appears in Isaiah in chapter 4 in match with Numbers book 4 which uses the word *"tabernacle"* more than any other book of the Bible in the KJV; next, the word *"refuge"* first appears in Isaiah in chapter 4 in match with Numbers book 4 where *"refuge"* appears for the first time in the Bible in the KJV)

Isaiah chapter 5   Deuteronomy book 5

Isaiah 5:14 Therefore *hell* hath enlarged herself, and opened her mouth without measure:

Deuteronomy 32:22 For a fire is kindled in mine anger, and shall burn unto the lowest *hell,*

(special notes: the word *"hell"* first appears in Isaiah in chapter 5 in match with the first appearance of the word *"hell"* in the Bible which is in Deuteronomy book 5 in the KJV)

Isaiah 5:1,1 again,3,4,5,7,10 the word *"vineyard"* appears 7 times in the chapter in the KJV.

Deuteronomy 20:6; 22:9; 22:9 again; 23:24; 24:21; 28:30,39 the word *"vineyard"* appears 7 times in the book in the KJV.

Isaiah chapter 6   Joshua book 6

Isaiah 6:1 *In the year that king Uzziah died I saw also the Lord* sitting upon a throne,

Joshua 1:1 Now *after the death of Moses the servant of the LORD* it came to pass, that *the LORD spake unto Joshua*…

(special notes: Isaiah chapter 6 and Joshua book 6 begin in identical manner; next, note that in Isaiah 6:1-13, Isaiah appears before the Holy, Holy, Holy, Lord and in Joshua 5:13-15, Joshua appears before the holy captain of the host of the lord)

Isaiah 6:8 Also I heard the voice of the Lord, *saying*, Whom shall I send, and who will go for us? Then said I, *Here am I; send me*.

Joshua 1:16 And they answered Joshua, *saying*, All that thou commandest us we will do, and *whithersoever thou sendest us, we will go*.

Isaiah chapter 7   Judges book 7

Isaiah 7:4 …fear not, neither be fainthearted for the *two tails* of these smoking *firebrands*…

Judges 15:4 And Samson went and caught three hundred foxes, and took *firebrands*, and turned tail to tail, and put a firebrand in the midst between *two tails*.

(special notes: the words *"two tails"* occurs only in Isaiah chapter 7 and Judges book 7 in the entire Bible KJV for a perfect match; next, note both occurrences are in the verse 4 slot)

Isaiah 7:14 Behold, a virgin shall *conceive, and bear a son,* and shall call his name Immanuel.

Judges 13:3 thou shalt *conceive, and bear a son.*

Judges 13:5 thou shalt *conceive, and bear a son.*

Judges 13:7 thou shalt *conceive, and bear a son.*

(special notes: the exact wording of *"conceive, and bear a son"* occurs only in Isiah chapter 7 and Judges book 7 in the entire Bible KJV for a perfect match)

Isaiah chapter 8   Ruth book 8

Isaiah 8:3 And I went unto the prophetess; and she conceived, and bare a son. Then said the LORD to me, Call his name *Maher–shalal–hash–baz*.

Ruth 2:23 So she kept fast by the maidens of *Boaz* to glean unto the end of barley harvest and of wheat harvest; and dwelt with her mother in law.

(special notes: the name *"Maher-shalal-has-baz"* means "make haste to the spoils." The name *"Boaz"* means "make haste." The name *"Boaz"* is at the end of the name *"Maher-shalal-has-baz."* Ruth made haste to the spoils (bread) by her gleaning in the field of Boaz)

Isaiah chapter 9   First Samuel book 9

Isaiah 9:7, 12 ...*David* ...*Philistines*

1 Samuel 21:9 And the priest said, The sword of Goliath the *Philistine*, whom thou slewest in the valley... And *David* said... give it me.

Isaiah 9:7 ...upon the throne of David, and upon his kingdom... the zeal of the Lord of hosts will perform this.

1 Samuel 16:13 Then Samuel took the horn of oil, and anointed him in the midst of his brethren: and the Spirit of the LORD came upon David from that day forward.

Isaiah chapter 10   Second Samuel book 10

Isaiah 10:17 And *the light of Israel* shall be for a fire, and his Holy One for a flame:

2 Samuel 21:17 Thou shalt go no more out with us to battle, that thou quench not *the light of Israel*.

(special notes: the exact wording of *"the light of Israel"* occurs only in Isaiah chapter 10 and Second Samuel book 10 in the entire Bible KJV for a perfect match; also note both are in verse 17 slot)

Isaiah 10:12,24,32 ...*Zion* ...*Zion* ...*Zion*

2 Samuel 5:7 Nevertheless David took the strong hold of *Zion*...

(special notes: the word *"Zion"* first occurs in the Bible in second Samuel book 10 in match with Isaiah chapter 10 in the KJV)

Isaiah chapter 11   First Kings book 11

Isaiah 11:14-16 ...*the Philistines* ...*Edom* ...*Moab* ...*the children of Ammon* ...*Assyria* ...*Israel* ...*the land of Egypt*.

1 Kings 4:21; 9:26; 11:7; 11:7 again; 11:25; 12:1; 12:28 ...*the Philistines* ...*Edom* ...*Moab* ...*the children of Ammon* ...*Syria* ...*Israel* ...*the land of Egypt*.

(special notes: these nations are grouped together in Isaiah 11 and in no other single chapter in the Bible and have the same chronological order as First Kings book 11 where all addresses match from low to high 4:21; 9:26; 11:7; 11:7 again; 11:25; 12:1; 12:28)

Isaiah chapter 12   Second Kings book 12

Isaiah 12:6 Cry out and shout, thou inhabitant of Zion: *for great is the Holy One of Israel* in the midst of thee.

2 Kings 5:15 Behold, now I know that *there is no God in all the earth, but in Israel*:

Isaiah chapter 13   First Chronicles book 13

Isaiah 13:12 I will make a man more precious than fine *gold; even* a man than *the gold*en wedge *of Ophir*.

1 Chronicles 29:4 *Even* three thousand talents of *gold*, of *the gold of Ophir*,

(special notes: Isaiah chapter 13 and First Chronicles book 13 contain the only two verses in the entire Bible to have the words *"even"* and *"gold* (2 x)"* and *"Ophir"* in them; Next, note that *"Ophir"* appears only one time In Isaiah and is in chapter 13 in match with First Chronicles book 13 in the Bible KJV)

Isaiah chapter 14   Second Chronicles book 14

Isaiah 14:28 In the year that king *Ahaz died* was this burden.

2 Chronicles 28:27 And *Ahaz slept with his fathers, and they buried him*

Isaiah chapter 15   Ezra book 15

Isaiah 15:2,3,4,5,8 …*weep* …howl …howl …*weeping* …cry…cry …cry… *weeping* …cry … cry …howling …howling

Ezra 3:12,13 But many of the priests and Levites and chief of the fathers, who were ancient men, that had seen the first house, when the foundation of this house was laid before their eyes, *wept* with a loud voice; and many shouted aloud for joy: So that the people could not discern the noise of the shout of joy from the noise of the *weeping* of the people:

(special notes: the inferiority of the new rebuilt temple compared to the superiority of Solomon's temple before it was destroyed was of major upset to the older generation who experienced it first hand)

Isaiah chapter 16   Nehemiah book 16

Isaiah 16:5 And in *mercy* shall the throne be established: and he shall sit upon it in truth in *the tabernacle of David*,

Nehemiah 1:5,11; 9:32; 13:22 …*mercy* …*mercy* …*mercy* …*mercy*

(special notes: Nehemiah petitioned God four times on the grounds of *"mercy"* for the end sake of rebuilding all that pertained to the temple, *"the tabernacle of David,"* including *"the city of David"* and *"the sepulchers of David"* and *"the commandment of David"* and *"the musical instruments of David"* and *"the city of David"* again, and *"the house of David"* and *"the commandment of David"* again, and *"the days of David"* in Nehemiah 3:15,16; 12:24,36,37,45,46)

Isaiah chapter 17   _Esther book 17_

Isaiah 17:14 This is the portion of them that spoil us, and _the lot_ of them that rob us.

Esther 3:7 they cast Pur, that is, _the lot_, before Haman...

Esther 9:24 and had cast Pur, that is, _the lot,_ to consume them...

(special notes: the word "_lot_" first occurs in Isaiah in chapter 17 in match with Esther book 17 in the KJV)

Isaiah chapter 18   _Job book 18_

Isaiah 18:1 _Woe_...

Job 10:15 _woe_ unto me... see thou mine affliction;

(special notes: the first word of Isaiah 18 is _"woe"_ according to the overwhelming theme of the _"woe"_ of Job book 18 in the KJV)

Isaiah 18:4,5 ..._herbs_ ..._dew_ ..._bud_

Job 38:25 ..._bud_ ..._herb_ ..._dew_

(special notes: Isaiah chapter 18 and Job book 18 are the only two places where the words _"herb"_ or _"herbs"_ and _"dew"_ and _"bud"_ appear in the same chapter in the Bible KJV)

CHAPTER 40

It Is Finished 2

But I Have Greater Witness Than That Of John: For The Works Which The Father Hath Given Me To Finish, The Same Works That I Do, Bear Witness Of Me, That The Father Hath Sent Me

John 5:36

Isaiah chapter 19   Psalms book 19

Isaiah 19:11,13 the princes of _Zoan_ are fools… The princes of _Zoan_ are become fools

Psalm 78:12,43 in the field of _Zoan_… in the field of _Zoan_

(special notes: Isaiah 19 and Psalms book 19 are the only two double references of _"Zoan"_ in a single chapter in the entire Bible KJV; next, note that the first appearance of the word _"Zoan"_ in Isaiah is in chapter 19 in match with Psalms book 19 in the KJV)

Isaiah 19:25 _Israel mine inheritance._

Psalm 78:71 *Israel his inheritance*.

(special notes: Isaiah 19 and Psalm book 19 are the only two places that call *"Israel"* by name as God's *"inheritance"* in the entire Bible KJV)

Isaiah chapter 20   *Proverbs book 20*

Isaiah 20:5,6 …afraid and ashamed of Ethiopia their *expectation*… such is our *expectation*, whither we flee for help to be delivered from the king of Assyria

Proverbs 11:7,23 When a wicked man dieth, his *expectation* shall perish… the *expectation* of the wicked is wrath.

(special notes: Isaiah 20 is the only usage of the word *"expectation"* in Isaiah in match with Proverbs book 20 in the KJV; next, note that Isaiah 20 and Proverbs book 20 are the only two double references of *"expectation"* in a single chapter in the entire Bible KJV)

Isaiah chapter 21   *Ecclesiastes book 21*

Isaiah 21:1 As *whirlwinds* in *the south* pass through;

Ecclesiastes 1:6 The *wind* goeth toward *the south*, and turneth about unto the north; it *whirl*eth about continually, and the wind returneth again according to his *circuits*.

(special notes: the *"whirlwinds"* of Isaiah chapter 21 are winds that go in circles in match with *"circuits"* of Ecclesiastes book 21 of the Bible KJV)

Isaiah 21:7,9,12 …a couple of horsemen …a couple of horsemen …is fallen, is fallen …*the morning cometh, and also the night* … enquire, enquire … return, come

The 1611 King James Bible

Ecclesiastes 1:1, 5 vanity of vanities; all is vanity… The *sun also ariseth, and the sun goeth down*, and hasteth to his place where he arose.

(special notes: the repetitious nature of the verbiage in Isaiah chapter 21 is in match with the main theme of vain repetition in Ecclesiastes book 21 of the Bible KJV)

Isaiah chapter 22   Song Of Solomon book 22

Isaiah 22:4 Therefore said I, *Look away from me*; I will weep bitterly, labour not to comfort me, because of *the spoiling of the daughter* of my people.

Song Of Solomon 1:6 *Look not upon me*, because I am black, because the sun hath looked upon me: my mother's children were angry with me; they made me the keeper of the vineyards; but *mine own vineyard have I not kept*.

Isaiah 22:24 …even to all the vessels of *flagons*

Song Of Solomon 2:5 Stay me with *flagons*…

(special notes: the first usage of the word *"flagons"* in the Bible is in Song Of Solomon book 22 in match with the first usage of the word *"flagons"* in Isaiah which is in chapter 22 in the KJV)

Isaiah chapter 23   Isaiah book 23

Isaiah 23:1,14 Howl, ye *ships of Tarshish*; for it is *laid waste*… Howl, ye *ships of Tarshish*: for your strength is *laid waste*.

Isaiah 2:12,16,17 For the day of the LORD of hosts shall be upon every one that is proud and lofty, and upon every one that is lifted up… And upon all the *ships of Tarshish*… and the haughtiness of men shall be *made low*:

(special notes: nearly all the words making up Isaiah chapter 23 can be found somewhere in Isaiah book 23 in the Bible KJV. Example *"virgin"*

Isaiah 23:12 and *"a virgin shall conceive, and bear a son, and shall call his name Immanuel"* Isaiah 7:14)

Isaiah chapter 24   Jeremiah book 24

Isaiah 24:16 …yea, the treacherous dealers have *dealt very treacherously*.

Jeremiah 5:11 the house of Judah have *dealt very treacherously* against me…

(special notes: The phrase *"dealt very treacherously"* Isaiah chapter 24 and Jeremiah book 24 are the only two places where this is found in the Bible KJV)

Isaiah 24:17 *Fear, and the pit, and the snare,* are *upon thee, O inhabitant of* the earth.

Jeremiah 48:43 *Fear, and the pit, and the snare,* shall be *upon thee, O inhabitant of* Moab, saith the LORD.

(special notes: this is a quotation of Isaiah chapter 24 found word for word in Jeremiah book 24 of the Bible KJV)

Isaiah chapter 25   Lamentations book 25

Isaiah 25:1 thy counsels of old are *faithfulness*

Lamentations 3:23 great is thy *faithfulness*

Isaiah 25:8 the Lord GOD will wipe away *tears* from off all *faces*;

Lamentations 1:2 She weepeth sore in the night, and her *tears* are on her *cheeks*:

Isaiah chapter 26   Ezekiel book 26

Isaiah 26:19 *Thy dead men shall live*, together with my dead body shall they arise. Awake and sing, *ye that dwell in dust*: for thy dew is as the dew of herbs, and *the earth shall cast out the dead*.

Ezekiel 37:4-6, 9, 12-14 *O ye dry bones*, hear the word of the LORD. Thus saith the Lord GOD unto these bones; Behold, I will cause breath to enter into you, and *ye shall live*: And I will lay sinews upon you, and will bring up flesh upon you, and cover you with skin, and put breath in you, and *ye shall live*; and ye shall know that I am the LORD… *that they may live*… *and they lived*… I will *open your graves*, and cause you to come up *out of your graves*… And ye shall know that I am the LORD, when I have *opened your graves*, O my people, and brought you up *out of your graves*… *and ye shall live*…

Isaiah chapter 27   Daniel book 27

Isaiah 27:1 In that day the LORD with his sore and great and strong sword shall punish *leviathan* the piercing *serpent*, even *leviathan* that crooked *serpent*; and he shall *slay* the *dragon* that is in *the sea*.

Daniel 7:3,11 And *four great beasts* came up from *the sea*, diverse one from another… I beheld even till the beast was *slain*…

Isaiah 27:9 By this therefore shall the iniquity of Jacob be *purged*; and this is all the fruit *to take away his sin*;

Daniel 11:35 to try them, and to *purge*, and *to make them white*, even to the time of the end:

Isaiah 27:9 …as *chalkstones* that are beaten in sunder, the groves and *images shall not stand up*.

Daniel 2:34 …a stone was cut out without hands, which *smote the image upon his feet* that were of iron and *clay*, and *brake them to pieces*.

Isaiah chapter 28   Hosea book 28

Isaiah 28:1,3 Woe to the crown of *pride*, to the drunkards of *Ephraim*... The crown of *pride*, the drunkards of *Ephraim*...

Hosea 5:5 And the *pride* of Israel doth testify to his face: therefore shall Israel and *Ephraim* fall in their iniquity;

(special notes: outside of the book of Isaiah, the words *"pride"* and *"Ephraim"* only appear in a single verse together in Hosea book 28 in match with Isaiah chapter 28 in the Bible KJV)

Isaiah 28:24 Doth the plowman *plow* all day to sow? doth he open and *break* the *clods* of his ground?

Hosea 10:11 Judah shall *plow*, and Jacob shall *break* his *clods*.

(special notes: the words *"plow"* and *"break"* and *"clods"* only appear in a single verse together in Isaiah chapter 28 and Hosea book 28 in the entire Bible KJV; next, note that both Isaiah chapter 28 and Hosea book 28 are pointed at the nation of Ephraim)

Isaiah chapter 29   Joel book 29

Isaiah 29:1,2,7,8 ...*Ariel* ...*Ariel* ...*Ariel* ...*Ariel* ...*Ariel* ...*mount Zion*

Joel 2:32; 3:1,6,16,17,20 ...*Jerusalem* ...*Jerusalem* ...*Jerusalem* ...*Jerusalem* ...*Jerusalem* ...*Jerusalem*

(special notes: the names *"Ariel"* and *"mount Zion"* both refer to *"Jerusalem"* and occur six times in Isaiah chapter 29 in match with the six times in Joel book 29 of the Bible KJV)

Isaiah 29:7,8,10,11 ...shall be as a *dream* of a night *vision*... as when an hungry man *dreameth*... or as when a thirsty man *dreameth*... For *the LORD hath poured out upon you the spirit* of deep sleep... the *prophets* and your rulers... And the _vision_ of all is become unto you as the words of a book that is sealed...

Joel 2:28, 29 ..._I will pour out my spirit_ upon all flesh; and your sons and your daughters shall _prophesy_, your old men shall _dream dreams_, your young men shall see _visions_: And also upon the servants and upon the handmaids in those days will _I pour out my spirit_.

Isaiah chapter 30   _Amos book 30_

Isaiah 30:10 Which say to the _seers_... _Prophesy not unto us_ right things, speak unto us smooth things, prophesy deceits:

Amos 7:12 O thou _seer_, go, flee thee away into the land of Judah, and there eat bread, and _prophesy there_:

Isaiah 30:27 ...the LORD cometh from far... his tongue as a _devouring fire_:

Amos 1:4,7,10,12,14; 2:2,5; 5:6; 7:4 ..._fire_ ..._devour_ ..._fire_ ..._devour_ ..._fire_ ..._devour_ ..._fire_ ..._devour_ ..._fire_ ..._devour_ ..._fire_ ..._devour_ ..._fire_ ..._devour_ ..._fire_ ..._devour_ ..._fire_ ..._devoured_

Isaiah 30:27, 28 ...the LORD cometh from far... to _sift_ the nations with the _sieve_...

Amos 9:9 ...all nations, like as corn is _sifted_ in a _sieve_...

(special notes: Isaiah chapter 30 in match with Amos book 30 are the only two places where the word _"sieve"_ appear in the entire Bible KJV)

Isaiah chapter 31   _Obadiah book 31_

Isaiah 31:4 ...so shall the LORD of hosts come down to fight for _mount Zion_,

Obadiah 17 But upon _mount Zion_ shall be deliverance,

(special notes: by word count Isaiah chapter 31 is the fifth shortest chapter of the sixty-six chapters of the book of Isaiah in match with Obadiah which is by word count the fifth shortest book of the sixty-six books of the Bible KJV)

Isaiah chapter 32   Jonah book 32

Isaiah 32:2 And _a man shall be as an hiding place_ from the _wind_, and a covert from the _tempest_;

Jonah 1:4,12 But the LORD sent out a great _wind_ into the sea, and there was a mighty _tempest_ in the sea, so that the ship was like to be broken... And he said unto them, _Take me up, and cast me forth into the sea; so shall the sea be calm unto you_: for I know that for my sake this great tempest is upon you.

(special notes: in Isaiah chapter 32 a man is prophesied _"as an"_ hiding place from the _"wind"_ and _"tempest"_ in match with a man who was a hiding place from the _"wind"_ and _"tempest"_ in Jonah book 32 of the Bible KJV)

Isaiah 32:11 ..._strip you_, and make you bare, and _gird sackcloth_ upon your loins.

Jonah 3:5, 6 So the people of Nineveh... _put on sackcloth_... For word came unto the king of Nineveh... and he _laid his robe from him_, and _covered him with sackcloth_...

Isaiah chapter 33   Micah book 33

Isaiah 33:9 ...and _Bashan_ and _Carmel_ shake off their fruits.

Micah 7:14 ...in the midst of _Carmel_: let them feed in _Bashan_...

Isaiah 33:20 _Look upon Zion_, the city of our solemnities: thine _eyes_ shall see Jerusalem…

Micah 4:11 Let her be defiled, and let our _eye look upon Zion_.

(special notes: Isaiah chapter 33 in match with Micah book 33 are the only two places where the phrase *"look upon Zion"* appear in the entire Bible KJV)

Isaiah chapter 34   Nahum book 34

Isaiah 34:1, 2 …let _the earth_ hear, and _all that is therein_; _the world, and all things that come forth of it_. For the _indignation of the LORD_ is upon all nations, and _his fury_ upon all their armies:

Nahum 1:5, 6 …and _the earth_ is burned at his presence, yea, _the world, and all that dwell therein_. Who can stand before _his indignation_? and who can abide in the fierceness of his anger? _his fury_ is poured out like fire…

Isaiah 34:3 Their _slain_ also shall be cast out, and their stink shall come up out of their _carcases_…

Nahum 3:3 and there is a multitude of _slain_, and a great number of _carcases_;

(special notes: Isaiah chapter 34 in match with Nahum book 34 are the only two places where the words *"slain"* and *"carcases"* appear in a single verse together in the entire Bible KJV)

Isaiah chapter 35   Habakkuk book 35

Isaiah 35:1,2 …the desert shall _rejoice_, and _blossom_ as the rose. It shall _blossom_ abundantly, and _rejoice_ even with _joy_ and singing

Habakkuk 3:17,18 Although the fig tree shall not _blossom_… Yet I will _rejoice_ in the LORD, I will _joy_ in the God of my salvation.

(special notes: the words *"rejoice"* and *"blossom"* only appear together in a single book and even tighter in a single chapter and even tighter in back to back verses in Isaiah chapter 35 and Habakkuk book 35 in the entire Bible KJV; Adding the word *"joy"* yields the same result)

Isaiah chapter 36   Zephaniah book 36

Isaiah 36:11 Speak, I pray thee, unto thy servants in the Syrian language; for we understand it: and speak not to us in the Jews' *language*…

Zephaniah 3:9 For then will I turn to the people a pure *language*, that they may all call upon the name of the LORD…

Isaiah 36:15 Neither let Hezekiah make you *trust in the LORD*,

Zephaniah 3:2 …*she trusted not in the LORD*;

CHAPTER 41

IT IS FINISHED 3

I HAVE GLORIFIED THEE ON THE EARTH:
I HAVE FINISHED THE WORK WHICH
THOU GAVEST ME TO DO

JOHN 17:4

Isaiah chapter 37   Haggai book 37

Isaiah 37:31 And the <u>remnant</u> that is escaped of the house of Judah shall again take root downward, and bear fruit upward:

Haggai 1:14 And the LORD stirred up the spirit of Zerubbabel the son of Shealtiel, governor of Judah, and the spirit of Joshua the son of Josedech, the high priest, and the spirit of all the <u>remnant</u> of the people; and they came and did work in the house of the LORD of hosts, their God,

(Special notes: Isaiah chapter 37 prophesies the *"remnant"* who escaped alive the fall of Judah to Babylon in match with Haggai book 37 which lists some of this *"remnant"* who fulfill Isaiah's prophecy)

Isaiah 37:38 And it came to pass… <u>*his sons smote him with the sword*</u>;

Haggai 2:22 And I will overthrow the throne of kingdoms… every one *by the sword of his brother*.

Isaiah chapter 38   Zechariah book 38

Isaiah 38:3 …*Remember now, O LORD*, I beseech thee…

Zechariah the name Zechariah means *the LORD remembers*

Isaiah 38:22 What is the *sign* that I shall go up to *the house of the LORD*?

Zechariah 9:9 behold, thy King cometh unto thee …lowly, and riding upon an ass, and upon a colt the foal of an ass.

(special notes: Hezekiah's personal question in Isaiah chapter 38 is prophetically answered in the *"sign"* of Messiah making His triumphant entry up to the *"house of the LORD"* in Zechariah book 38 of the Bible)

Isaiah chapter 39   Malachi book 39

Isaiah 39:3-6 Then came Isaiah the prophet unto king Hezekiah, and said unto him, What said these men? and from whence came they unto thee? And Hezekiah said, They are come from a far country unto me, even from Babylon. Then said he, What have they seen in thine house? And Hezekiah answered, All that is in mine house have they seen: there is nothing among my treasures that I have not shewed them. Then said Isaiah to Hezekiah, Hear the word of the LORD of hosts: Behold, the days come, that all that is in thine house, and that which thy fathers have laid up in store until this day, shall be carried to Babylon: nothing shall be left, saith the LORD.

Malachi 3:8 *Will a man rob God*? Yet ye have robbed me.

(special notes: Isaiah chapter 39 reveals the answer to the question *"will a man rob God?"* asked in Malachi book 39 of the Bible and the answer is "Yes, King Nebuchadnezzar will rob the house of the LORD")

Isaiah chapter 40   Matthew book 40

Isaiah 40:1, 2 *Comfort ye, comfort ye* my people… Speak ye *comfort*ably to *Jerusalem*… for she hath received of the LORD'S hand *double* for all *her sins*.

Matthew 23:37; 5:4 O *Jerusalem, Jerusalem, thou that killest* the prophets… Blessed are they that mourn: for they shall be *comfort*ed.

(special notes: Jesus fulfills the opening words of Isaiah chapter 40 with his opening sermon on the mount in Matthew book 40 of the Bible)

Isaiah 40:3 The voice of him that crieth in the wilderness, *Prepare ye the way of the LORD, make straight* in the desert *a highway* for our God.

Matthew 3:3 For this is he that was spoken of by the prophet Esaias, saying, The voice of one crying in the wilderness, *Prepare ye the way of the Lord, make his paths straight*.

Isaiah 40:8 …the flower fadeth: *but the word of our God shall stand for ever*.

Matthew 24:35 Heaven and earth shall pass away, *but my words shall not pass away*.

Isaiah 40:9 O Zion, that bringest *good tidings*…O Jerusalem, that bringest *good tidings*,

Matthew Matthew ushers in the gospel which means *good tidings*

Isaiah chapter 41   Mark book 41

Isaiah 41:7 So the *carpenter* encouraged the goldsmith…

Mark 6:3 Is not this the *carpenter*, the son of Mary…

(special notes: Mark book 41 in match with Isaiah chapter 41 is the only place outside of Isaiah where the word *"carpenter"* appears in the entire Bible KJV)

Isaiah 41:14 Fear not, <u>*thou worm Jacob*</u>, and ye men of Israel; I will help thee, saith the LORD…

Mark 14:35 And he went forward a little, and <u>*fell on the ground*</u>, and prayed that, if it were possible, the hour might pass from him.

(special notes: on the night before Jesus was sacrificed for Jacob He cast Himself down to the ground assuming the place and figure of the *"worm"* soon to be squished; this act only takes place in Mark book 41 in match with Isaiah chapter 41)

Isaiah 41:26 <u>*Who*</u> hath declared from the beginning, that we may know?

Mark 13:23 And <u>*Jesus*</u> answering them began to say… I have foretold you all things.

Isaiah chapter 42 *Luke book 42*

Isaiah 42:6 …and give thee for a covenant of the people, <u>*for a light of the Gentiles*</u>;

Luke 2:32 <u>*A light to lighten the Gentiles*</u>, and the glory of thy people Israel.

Isaiah 42:18 <u>*Hear, ye deaf*</u>; and <u>*look, ye blind*</u>, that ye may see.

Luke 7:22 …<u>*the blind see*</u>… <u>*the deaf hear*</u>,

Isaiah 42:20 <u>*Seeing*</u> many things, but <u>*thou observest not*</u>; opening the <u>*ears*</u>, but <u>*he heareth not*</u>.

Luke 8:10 …that <u>*seeing they might not see*</u>, and <u>*hearing they might not understand*</u>.

Isaiah chapter 43   *John book 43*

Isaiah 43:1 …I have redeemed thee, *I have called thee by thy name; thou art mine*.

John 10:3 … and *he calleth his own sheep by name*, and leadeth them out.

Isaiah 43:10 …*that ye may know and believe* me, and understand that I am he:

John 10:38 …*that ye may know, and believe*, that the Father is in me, and I in him.

(special notes: Isaiah chapter 43 in match with John book 43 are the only two places where the phrase *"that ye may know, and believe"* appear in the entire Bible KJV)

Isaiah 43:10 …understand that *I am he*: before me there was no God formed, neither shall there be after me.

John 8:24,28; 13:19; 18:8 …if ye believe not that *I am he*, ye shall die in your sins …When ye have lifted up the Son of man, then shall ye know that *I am he* …when it is come to pass, ye may believe that *I am he* …I have told you that *I am he*:

Isaiah 43:12 …*I am God*.

John 10:33 …For a good work we stone thee not; but for blasphemy; and because that thou, being a man, *makest thyself God*.

Isaiah 43:13 …*and there is none that can deliver out of my hand*:

John 10:29 …*and no man is able to pluck them out of my Father's hand*.

Isaiah chapter 44   *Acts book 44*

Isaiah 44:3,8 I will *pour my spirit upon thy seed*… *ye are even my witnesses*.

Acts 1:8 But ye shall receive power, after that *the Holy Ghost is come upon you*: and *ye shall be witnesses unto me*…

(special notes: *"ye are even my witnesses"* and *"ye shall be witnesses unto me"* both occur in the verse 8 slot of Isaiah chapter 44 and Acts book 44 in the Bible)

Isaiah 44:24 I am *the LORD* that *maketh* *all things*; that stretcheth forth the *heaven*s alone; that spreadeth abroad the *earth* by myself;

Acts 17:24 *God* that *made* the world and *all things* therein, seeing that he is Lord of *heaven* and *earth*…

(special notes: both verses occur in the verse 24 slot of Isaiah chapter 44 and Acts book 44 in the Bible)

Isaiah chapter 45   *Romans book 45*

Isaiah 45:4 For *Jacob* my servant's sake, and *Israel* mine *elect*…

Romans 11:26, 28 *Israel*… *Jacob*… as touching the *elect*ion, they are beloved…

Isaiah 45:9 Woe unto *him that striveth with his Maker*! …*Shall the clay say to him that fashioneth it, What makest thou?*

Romans 9:20, 21 Nay but, O man, who art *thou that repliest against God? Shall the thing formed say to him that formed it, Why hast thou made me thus?*

Isaiah 45:17 ye *shall not be ashamed* nor confounded world without end.

Romans 10:11 For the scripture saith, Whosoever believeth on him *shall not be ashamed*.

(special notes: Romans book 45 in match with Isaiah chapter 45 is the only place in the N.T. where the phrase *"shall not be ashamed"* appears in the entire Bible KJV)

Isaiah 45:17 But *Israel shall be saved*...

Romans 11:26 And so all *Israel shall be saved*:

(special notes: Isaiah chapter 45 in match with Romans book 45 are the only two places where the phrase *"Israel shall be saved"* appear in the entire Bible KJV)

Isaiah 45:23 *I have sworn by myself, the word is gone out of my mouth*... That *unto me every knee shall bow, every tongue shall swear.*

Romans 14:11 For it is written, *As I live, saith the Lord, every knee shall bow to me, and every tongue shall confess* to God.

Isaiah 45:25 In the LORD shall all the seed of Israel be *justified*,

Romans The book of Romans is the official book of *justification* in the Bible

Isaiah chapter 46   First Corinthians book 46

Isaiah 46:6, 7 ...he maketh it *a god* ...one shall cry unto him, yet *can he not answer*...

1 Corinthians 12:2 Ye know that ye were Gentiles, carried away unto these *dumb idols*,

Isaiah 46:9 I am God, and *there is none else*; I am *God*, and there is *none like me*,

1 Corinthians 8:4 there is *none other God but one*.

Isaiah 46:10 Declaring the end from the beginning, and from ancient times the things that are not yet done,

1 Corinthians 2:9 Eye hath not seen, nor ear heard… the things which God hath prepared

(special notes: Isaiah chapter 46 describes the God created genetic line of chromosomal life from conception into grey haired old age in verses three and four *"borne by me from the belly, which are carried from the womb: And even to your old age I am he; and even to hoar hairs will I carry you"* according to First Corinthians book 46 representing the 46 chromosomes of the human body; see First Corinthians 3:16; 6:19)

Isaiah chapter 47   Second Corinthians book 47

Isaiah 47:3 Thy *nakedness shall be uncovered*, yea, thy shame shall be seen:

2 Corinthians 5:2, 3 …If so be that being clothed we shall not *be found naked*…

Isaiah 47:1 Come down, and sit in the dust, O *virgin* daughter of Babylon…

2 Corinthians 11:2 …that I may present you as a chaste *virgin* to Christ.

Isaiah chapter 48   Galatians book 48

Isaiah 48:8 …and wast *called* a *transgressor from the womb*.

Galatians 1:15 …who separated me *from my mother's womb*, and *called* me…

(special notes: first reference is Jacob and second reference is Paul who in the next chapter calls himself a *"transgressor"* see 2:18)

Isaiah 48:16,17,18,21,22 the Lord GOD, and *his Spirit*… which *leadeth thee*… then had thy *peace* been as a river… And they thirsted not *when he led them through the deserts: he caused the waters to flow out of the rock for them*:... There is *no peace*, saith the LORD, unto *the wicked*.

Galatians 5:16,17,18,21,22 Walk in *the Spirit*, and ye shall not fulfil the lust of the flesh... For *the flesh* lusteth against *the Spirit*... But if ye be *led of the Spirit*... as I have also told you *in time past*... But the fruit of *the Spirit* is love, joy, *peace*...

(special notes: the above matches all occur in the verse slots 16,17,18,21,22 in Isaiah chapter 48 and Galatians book 48 in the Bible KJV; next, note *"when he led them through the deserts: he caused the waters to flow out of the rock for them"* from Isaiah chapter 48 is in match with the words *"in time past"* from Galatians book 48 as it recalls history, i.e. *"in time past"*)

Isaiah chapter 49   Ephesians book 49

Isaiah 49:2 ...he hath made my *mouth* like a sharp *sword*;

Ephesians 6:17 ...the *sword* of the Spirit, which is the *word* of God:

Isaiah 49:5 yet shall I be *glorious in the eyes of the LORD*,

Ephesians 1:4, 6, 12, 18 According as *he hath chosen us in him* before the foundation of the world... To the praise of the *glory* of *his* grace... That we should be to the praise of *his glory*... the *glory* of *his* inheritance...

Isaiah chapter 50   Philippians book 50

Isaiah 50:5, 6 The Lord GOD hath *opened mine ear,* and I was *not rebellious,* neither turned away back. I gave my back to the smiters, and my cheeks to them that plucked off the hair: I hid not my face from shame and spitting.

Philippians 2:8 ...took upon him the form of *a servant*... and became *obedient* unto death, even the death of the cross.

(special notes: *"opened mine ear"* refers to the practice of piercing the ear of a *"servant"* unto servitude for life; see Ex. 21:6; Deut. 15:17)

Isaiah 50:10 Who is among you that <u>*feareth*</u> the LORD, that <u>*obeyeth*</u> the voice of his <u>*servant*</u>...

Philippians 2:7,12 ...took upon him the form of a <u>*servant*</u>... as ye have always <u>*obeyed*</u>... work out your own salvation with <u>*fear*</u> and trembling.

<u>Isaiah chapter 51</u>   *<u>Colossians book 51</u>*

Isaiah 51:3 joy and gladness shall be found therein, <u>*thanksgiving*</u>, and the voice of melody.

Colossians 1:3,12; 2:7; 3:15,17; 4:2 We give <u>*thanks*</u> to God and the Father... Giving <u>*thanks*</u> unto the Father... abounding therein with <u>*thanksgiving*</u>... be ye <u>*thankful*</u> ...giving <u>*thanks*</u> to God and the Father... watch... with <u>*thanksgiving*</u>;

(special notes: Isaiah chapter 51 in match with the major theme of *"thanksgiving"* in Colossians book 51 is the only place in the entirety of the book of Isaiah KJV that has any form of the word *thank, thanks, thanked, thanking, thankful, thankfulness, thanksgiving,* etc.)

Isaiah 51:13 And forgettest <u>the LORD thy maker, that hath stretched forth the heavens, and laid the foundations of the earth</u>; and hast feared continually every day because of <u>the fury of the oppressor</u>, as if he were <u>ready to destroy</u>? and where is <u>the fury of the oppressor</u>?

Colossians 1:16 For <u>by him were all things created, that are in heaven, and that are in earth</u>, visible and <u>*invisible*</u>, whether they be <u>*thrones*</u>, or <u>*dominions*</u>, or <u>*principalities*</u>, or <u>*powers*</u>:

(special notes: *"thrones, dominions, principalities, powers"* refer to *"the oppressor"* which is *"ready to destroy"* as defined by Daniel 7:9, 27 and Ephesians 6:12)

CHAPTER 42

IT IS FINISHED 4

WHEN JESUS THEREFORE HAD RECEIVED
THE VINEGAR, HE SAID, IT IS FINISHED:
AND HE BOWED HIS HEAD, AND
GAVE UP THE GHOST

JOHN 19:30

Isaiah chapter 52   First Thessalonians book 52

Isaiah 52:2 _Shake thyself from the dust; arise_...

1 Thessalonians 4:16 For the Lord himself shall descend from heaven with a shout, with the voice of the archangel, and with the trump of God: and _the dead in Christ shall rise_ first:

Isaiah 52:11 ..._be ye clean_, that bear the _vessels_ of the LORD.

1 Thessalonians 4:4 That every one of you should know how to possess his _vessel_ in _sanctification_...

Isaiah 52:1,11 Awake, awake... Depart ye, depart ye...

1 Thessalonians 5:7,22; 4:3 ...sleep sleep... abstain... abstain

Isaiah chapter 53   Second Thessalonians book 53

Isaiah 53:1 Who hath *believed* *our report*?

2 Thessalonians 1:10 because *our testimony* among you was *believed*

Isaiah 53:1 ...and *to whom* is *the arm of the LORD* revealed?

2 Thessalonians 1:8,9 *on them* that know not God, and that obey not the gospel of our Lord Jesus Christ: Who shall be *punished with everlasting destruction* from the presence of the Lord, and from the glory of his power;

Isaiah chapter 54   First Timothy book 54

Isaiah 54:4 thou shalt forget the *shame* of thy *youth*,

1 Timothy 4:12 Let no man despise thy *youth*; but be thou an *example*...

(special notes: Isaiah chapter 54 *"forget the shame of thy youth"* fulfilled in First Timothy book 54 *"an example"* of *"youth"*)

Isaiah 54:4 thou... shalt not remember the *reproach* of thy *widowhood* any more.

1 Timothy 5:3,4,5 *Honour widows* that are *widows* indeed... but if any *widow* have children... now she that is a *widow* indeed...

(special notes: Isaiah chapter 54 *"not remember the reproach of thy widowhood"* fulfilled in First Timothy book 54 *"Honour widows"*)

Isaiah 54:16,17 Behold, I have created *the smith* that bloweth the coals in the fire... and I have created *the waster to destroy*. No weapon that is formed against thee shall prosper; and every tongue that shall *rise against thee* in judgment *thou shalt condemn*. This is the heritage of *the servants of the LORD*, and their righteousness is of me, saith the LORD.

1 Timothy 1:20 Of whom is *Hymenaeus* and *Alexander*; whom *I have delivered unto Satan*, that they may learn not to blaspheme.

(special notes: in 2 Timothy 2:17 *"Hymenaeus"* is called a canker worm which eats away and is therefore a *"waster to destroy;"* in 2 Timothy 4:14 *"Alexander"* is called a copper *"smith;"* Paul, according to *"heritage"* as one of *"the servants of the LORD"* on account of their *"blaspheme"* acted to *"condemn"* them both *"whom I have delivered unto Satan"*)

Isaiah chapter 55   Second Timothy book 55

Isaiah 55:10 For as the *rain* cometh down, and the *snow* from heaven…

2 Timothy 4:21 Do thy diligence to come before *winter*.

Isaiah 55:10 …*bread to the eater*:

2 Timothy 3:15 *from a child thou hast known the holy scriptures*,

Isaiah 55:11 So shall *my word be that goeth forth out of my mouth*…

2 Timothy 3:16 *All scripture is given by inspiration of God*,

Isaiah 55:11 …*it shall accomplish that which I please*,

2 Timothy 3:16 and *is profitable for doctrine, for reproof, for correction, for instruction in righteousness*:

Isaiah 55:11 …*it shall prosper in the thing whereto I sent it*.

2 Timothy 3:17 *That the man of God may be perfect*…

Isaiah chapter 56   *Titus book 56*

Isaiah 56:10 *His watchmen* are *blind*: they are all *ignorant*, they are all *dumb*...

Titus 1:5,9 *elders*... that he may be *able by sound doctrine both to exhort and to convince*

Isaiah 56:10, 11 *His watchmen*... Yea, *they are greedy* dogs which *can never have enough*, and they are *shepherds* that cannot understand: they all look to their own way, *every one for his gain*, from his quarter.

Titus 1:5, 7 *elders*... *not given to filthy lucre*... *just*... *temperate*

Isaiah 56:10, 11, 12 *His watchmen*... *shepherds*... Come ye, say they, *I will fetch wine*, and *we will fill ourselves with strong drink*;

Titus 1:5, 7, 8 *elders*... *not given to wine*... *sober*

Isaiah chapter 57   *Philemon book 57*

Isaiah 57:12 I will declare thy righteousness, and thy works; for *they shall not profit thee.*

Philemon 10,11 *Onesimus*... Which in time past was to thee *unprofitable*, but now *profitable* to thee and to me:

(special notes: the name *"Onesimus"* means profitable)

Isaiah 57:19 *Peace, peace to him that is far off, and to him that is near*...

Philemon 10 *I beseech thee* for my son Onesimus, whom I have begotten in my bonds:

(special notes: Paul was sending a letter to make *"peace"* between the runaway servant Onesimus who was with Paul *"near"* and Onesimus' master Philemon who was *"far off"*)

Isaiah chapter 58   Hebrews book 58

Isaiah 58:2 ...they take delight in *approaching* to God.

Hebrews 10:25 exhorting one another: and so much the more, as ye see the day *approaching*.

(special notes: Isaiah chapter 58 in match with Hebrews book 58 are the only two places where the word *"approaching"* is used in the entire Bible KJV)

Isaiah 58:12 ...thou shalt raise up the foundations of *many generations*;

Hebrews 11:4,5,7,8,9,11,22,23,31,32 By faith *Abel*... By faith *Enoch*... By faith *Noah*... By faith *Abraham*... *Isaac* and *Jacob*... Through faith also *Sara*... By faith *Joseph*... By faith *Moses*... *Rahab*... *Gedeon*... *Barak*... *Samson*... *Jephthae*... *David*... *Samuel*...

Isaiah chapter 59   James book 59

Isaiah 59:3 For your hands are *defiled* with blood... your *tongue* hath muttered perverseness.

James 3:6 ...so is the *tongue* among our members, that it *defileth* the whole body...

(special notes: Isaiah chapter 59 in match with James book 59 are the only two places where the word *"tongue"* and the word *"defile, defileth or any form of the word, etc."* are used together in the same verse in the entire Bible KJV)

Isaiah 59:4 ...they *conceive* mischief, and *bring forth iniquity*.

James 1:15 when lust hath *conceived*, it *bringeth forth sin*:

Isaiah 59:6 ...neither shall they cover themselves with their *works*: their *works* are *works* of iniquity,

James 2:18 Thou hast faith, and I have _works_: shew me thy faith without thy _works_, and I will shew thee my faith by my _works_.

(special notes: Isaiah chapter 59 in match with James book 59 are the only two places where the word _"works"_ is used three times in the entire Bible KJV)

Isaiah chapter 60   First Peter book 60

Isaiah 60:2,3,16 …the _darkness_ shall cover the earth, and gross _darkness_ the people: but the LORD shall arise upon thee, and _his glory shall be seen upon thee_. And the Gentiles _shall come to thy light_… Thou shalt also _suck the milk_ of the Gentiles…

1 Peter 2:2,9; 4:14 As newborn babes, _desire the sincere milk_ of the word… that ye should shew forth the praises of him who hath called you _out of darkness into his marvellous light_… _for the spirit of glory and of God resteth upon you_:

Isaiah 60:6 …and they shall _shew forth the praises_ of the LORD.

1 Peter 2:9 that ye should _shew forth the praises_ of him who hath called you…

(special notes: Isaiah chapter 60 in match with 1 Peter book 60 are the only two places where the phrase _"shew forth the praises"_ is used in the entire Bible KJV)

Isaiah 60:15 Whereas thou hast been _forsaken and hated_… I will make thee an eternal _excellency_, a _joy_ of many generations.

1 Peter 4:13 inasmuch as ye are _partakers of Christ's sufferings_; that, when his glory shall be revealed, ye may be glad also with _exceeding joy_.

Isaiah chapter 61   Second Peter book 61

Isaiah 61:1 *The Spirit of the Lord GOD is upon me*; because *the LORD hath anointed me to preach*…

2 Peter 1:21 …*holy men of God spake* as they were *moved by the Holy Ghost*.

Isaiah 61:1 …to proclaim *liberty* to the *captives*…

2 Peter 2:19 While they promise them *liberty*, they themselves are the *servants of corruption*:

Isaiah chapter 62   First John book 62

Isaiah 62:2 And the Gentiles shall *see thy righteousness*…

1 John 3:2 …we shall *see him as he is*.

Isaiah 62:2 …and *thou shalt be called by a new name*, which the mouth of *the LORD shall name*.

1 John 3:1 Behold, what manner of love *the Father hath bestowed* upon us, that *we should be called the sons of God*:

Isaiah chapter 63   Second John book 63

Isaiah 63:8 Surely they are my people, *children that will not lie*:

2 John 4 I rejoiced greatly that I found of thy *children walking in truth*,

Isaiah 63:16 Doubtless thou art *our father*, though Abraham be ignorant of us, and Israel acknowledge us not: thou, O LORD, art *our father*, our redeemer; thy name is from everlasting.

2 John 9 He that abideth in the doctrine of Christ, he hath *both the Father* and the Son.

(special notes: the phrase *"both the Father"* in second John book 63 equates in match to the double usage of *"our father… our father"* in Isaiah chapter 63 KJV)

Isaiah chapter 64   *Third John book 64*

Isaiah 64:5 *Thou meetest him that rejoiceth and worketh righteousness, those that remember thee in thy ways*:

3 John 5,6 Beloved, *thou doest faithfully whatsoever thou doest to the brethren, and to strangers*; *Which have borne witness of thy charity* before the church…

Isaiah 64:7 *thou hast hid thy face* from us, and hast consumed us, because of *our iniquities*.

3 John 11 …*he that doeth evil* hath *not seen God*.

Isaiah chapter 65   *Jude book 65*

Isaiah 65:2 which *walketh*… *after their own thoughts*;

Jude 16,18 … *walking after their own lusts* …*walk after their own ungodly lusts*.

Isaiah 65:4 Which remain *among the graves*, and *lodge in the monuments*…

Jude 12 These are… *twice dead*…

(special notes: the phrase *"twice dead"* in Jude book 65 equates in match to the double usage of *"among the graves"* and *"lodge in the monuments (tomb stones)"* in Isaiah chapter 65 KJV)

Isaiah 65:5 Which say, *Stand by thyself, come not near to me*;

Jude 19 These be *they who separate themselves*,

Isaiah chapter 66   *Revelation book 66*

Isaiah 66:7 Before *she travailed*, *she brought forth*; before her *pain* came, she was *delivered* of *a man child*.

Revelation 12:2,5 And *she* being with child cried, *travailing* in birth, and *pained* to be *delivered*… And *she brought forth* *a man child*,

Isaiah 66:18 For *I know their works* and their thoughts:

Revelation 2:2,9,13,19; 3:1,8,15 *I know thy works*… *I know thy works*… *I know thy works*… *I know thy works*… *I know thy works*… *I know thy works*… *I know thy works*… *I know thy works*…

(special notes: The phrases *"I know their works"* and *"I know thy works"* are used only in Isaiah chapter 66 and Revelation book 66 in the entire Bible KJV)

Isaiah 66:24 And they shall go forth, *and look upon the carcases of the men that have transgressed against me*: for their worm shall not die, *neither shall their fire be quenched*;

Revelation 14:10,11 …and *he shall be tormented with fire and brimstone in the presence of the holy angels, and in the presence of the Lamb*: And *the smoke of their torment ascendeth up for ever and ever*:

Isaiah 66:22 For as *the new heavens and the new earth*, which I will make,

Revelation 21:1 And I saw *a new heaven and a new earth*: for the first heaven and the first earth were passed away;

POSTFACE

The LORD Shall Fight For You, And Ye Shall Hold Your Peace.

Exodus 14:14

In the end, most people who do not believe that God has seeded and raised up the King James Bible as His only begotten Bible do not want to believe.

Some of these people have invested their entire Christian lives building on a foundation that "God has not finished a specific single volume Bible." Of course, they have built their bibliology houses upon a foundation of sand which will one day, on this side of life or the other, be washed away.

If secretly in these people's hearts, their ministry is their identity, or their ministry is their pride, or their ministry is their life, it will be near impossible for them to self-condemn their foundation. Their own name is too much to walk away from for His name. However, if Christ alone is their life and desire, it is actually very easy to walk away from their bibliology houses built upon sand and rebuild their houses upon the rock of the true Bible. This is because wanting and willing go hand in hand. People get what they go after from the heart. If your heart is going after Christianity, you will get the broad way of counterfeit Bibles, and if your heart is going after Christ, you will find the narrow way of the King James Bible at any cost, *"Therefore whosoever heareth these sayings of mine, and doeth them, I will liken him unto a wise man, which built his house upon a rock (Matt. 7:24)."*

Some others still, are caught betwixt. Convicted of the KJV truth on the one hand, yet on the other hand insufficient in putting on the Lord Jesus Christ to take on the call of this truth. Like Pliable from Pilgrim's Progress, they are destined for the slough of despond once tribulation or persecution arises because of the word. After all, building your house on a new foundation means "new neighbors" or perhaps "no neighbors" at all. This can be a lonely and stripping season. And what if you run into the "old neighbors" and they ridicule you? *"Lest haply, after he hath laid the foundation, and is not able to finish it, all that behold it begin to mock him (Luke 14:29)."*

And some others finally, simply do not want to be bothered. They have neither the time nor the interest. They claim Christ, but they do not really care significantly about their houses they are building, let alone their foundations. For these, they are content to passively continue in the notion of Christianity all the days of their lives, living for themselves, while cleaving to a heavenly idea that God will work them out on the other side. Though they are warned and taught in all wisdom that 'now' they must be prepared to be presented to God (Col. 1:28), and 'now' are we the sons of God (1 John 3:2), their interest is dim and their attention is brief.

To any and all of these who are *"froward"* toward the King James Bible, God will be *"froward"* back in response and the King James Bible will continue to be concealed from Christians for the glory of God:

With the pure thou wilt shew thyself pure; and with the froward thou wilt shew thyself froward (Ps. 18:26)

Both the idea that God has finished a Bible, and the King James Bible itself, will be made *"unsavoury"* to such ones in heart:

With the pure thou wilt shew thyself pure; and with the froward thou wilt shew thyself unsavoury (2 Sam. 22:27)

And God will give them the room for unbelief they are looking for:

And he said, I will hide my face from them, I will see what their end shall be: for they are a very froward generation, children in whom is no faith (Deut. 32:20)

For you who are on the verge of putting your faith in God's finished Bible for the first time, I say with the Apostle Paul and the Spirit, *"And that, knowing the time, that now it is high time to awake out of sleep: for now is our salvation nearer than when we believed. The night is far spent, the day is at hand: let us therefore cast off the works of darkness, and let us put on the armour of light (Rom. 13:11,12)."*

For you who are already standing on the rock of the KJV, having escaped the mirage of false Bibles and overcome, wage the good fight of the faith in Christ Jesus and remain strong and supply the brethren in love, as the Lord will always keep a remnant who will bridge the gap of faith for the sake of the entire body of Christ, the strong bearing the weak: *"That we henceforth be no more children, tossed to and fro, and carried about with every wind of doctrine, by the sleight of men, and cunning craftiness, whereby they lie in wait to deceive; But speaking the truth in love, may grow up into him in all things, which is the head, even Christ: From whom the whole body fitly joined together and compacted by that which every joint supplieth, according to the effectual working in the measure of every part, maketh increase of the body unto the edifying of itself in love (Ephes. 4:14-16)."*

The author of this book can be reached at:

concealedfromchristians@gmail.com